Exploring Science

Penny Johnson
Mark Levesley

Edinburgh Gate
Harlow, Essex

Pearson Education
Edinburgh Gate
Harlow
Essex CM20 2JE

Fourth impression 2006
ISBN-10: 0-582-81899-0
ISBN-13: 978-0-582-81899-6

Original design concept by Pentacor plc, High Wycombe
Design concept adapted by Kamae Design, Oxford
Designed and produced by Kamae Design, Oxford
Printed in China SWTC/04

The publisher's policy is to use paper manufactured from sustainable forests.

Acknowledgements
We are grateful to the following for permission to reproduce photographs:

Action Plus, p16 *top*; AKG-Images, pp55 *top*, 30 *centre* (Lessing Archive/Erich Lessing); Alfa Remeo, p70 *top*; Ardea London Ltd, pp27 *top right* (Jim Bruton), 27 *bottom* (Robert T Smith), 28 *top* and 47 *top* (John Daniels), 33 (P Morris), 37 *top* (John Mason), 67 *left* (Francois Gohier); Arena Images, pp74 *bottom* (Pete Jones), 75 *top* (Hanya Chlala); Art Directors & TRIP, pp18 *top right* (D Clegg), 19 *centre left* and 38 *top right*, p54 *top* (NASA); Aviation Images, pp31 *centre right*, 56 *right*; A-Z Botanical/Bob Gibbons, p22 *right*; British Heart Foundation/Paul Mulcahy, p13 *top*; Channel 5/Guy Levy, p12; Trevor Clifford, pp8 *left*, 8 *right*, 19 *centre right*, 32 *bottom*, 37 *bottom*, 44, 46 *centre*, 48, 49, 57 *bottom*, 58, 62, 66 *left*, 66 *right*, 69 *right*, 72, 76 *top left*; CNES/Anne-Laure-HUET, 2001, p7 *top*; Corbis, pp11 (Jennie Woodcock /Reflections Photo Library), 27 *top left* (Kennan Ward), 30 *top* (Michael Freeman), 31 *top*, 41 *top* and 45 *left* (Roger Ressmeyer), 61 *bottom left* (Edifice), 61 *bottom right* (Paul Almasy), 63 *left* and 63 *right* (Mug Shots), 68 *right* (Amos Nachoum), 71 *bottom* (Jose Juis Pelaez), 74 *top* (Owen Franken), 76 top right (Tiziana and Gianni Baldizzone); Michael & Patricia Fogden pp 21 *bottom left*, 21 *bottom right*; GeoScience Features, p34 *centre*; Getty Images/Stone, pp 19 *top left*, 38 *top left*, 41 *bottom*, 45 *right*, 47 *bottom*; http://www.bnl.gov/bnlweb/pubaf/pr/1999/bnlpr092299.html, p77; Professor (VRC) Dr. Gunther von Hagens, Institut für Plastination, Heidelberg, Germany (www.bodyworlds.com), pp9 *bottom*, 15, 17 *top*; Kos Pictures, pp 31 *centre left*, 54 *bottom left*, 54 *bottom right*; Lebrecht Music Collection/Jim Four, p76 *bottom*; Mark Levesley, p40 *top*; Life File Photo Library, pp4 *top* and 70 *bottom* (Jan Suttle), 30 *bottom right*, 36 *centre* (Andrew Ward); Military Picture Library, pp71 *top*, Martin Mulcahy p34 *left*; Paul Mulcahy, pp4 *bottom*, 5, 6 *bottom*, 10, 16 *bottom*, 17 *bottom*, 19 *top right*, 21 *top*, 24, 30 *centre left*, 30 *centre right*, 34 *right*, 35, 37 *centre*, 39 *centre*, 40 *bottom*, 42 *bottom*, 43 *top*, 43 *centre*, 43 *bottom*, 45 *top*, 46 *bottom*, 47 *centre*; NASA, p55 *bottom left*; Natural Visions/Heather Angel, pp 18 *bottom left*, 18 *bottom right*, 53 *top*; Dr G. C. Nettmann p19 *bottom*; NHPA pp20 and 23 *top* (John Shaw), 22 *left* (Image Bank), 25 *top* (George Bernard), 29 *top* (ANT Photo Library), 29 *bottom* (Martin Wendler), 40 *centre* (Bill Wood), 61 *top* (Roger Tidman); Oxford Scientific Films, pp19 *centre* (Breck P Kent/AA), 28 *bottom*, 38 *centre*, 52 (Colin Monteath), 56 *left* (Ronald Toms), 64 *top left* (John Gerlach/AA), 64 *top centre* (Gene Bernard), 67 *bottom*; Philips, p36 *bottom left* and 36 *bottom right*; Popperfoto, pp 30 *bottom centre*, 32 *top* (Reuters), 75 *left* (Reuters/Jeff Mitchell), 53 *bottom left* (Reuters/Kipak Kumar); Redferns Music Picture Library, pp66 *top*, 68 *left* (Bob Huntbach), 75 *right* (Michel Linssen); Rex Features, pp39 *bottom* (Action Press), 42 *top*; Science Photo Library, pp13 *centre* (GJLP), 14 (Ouellette & Theroux), Publiphoto Diffusion, 18 *top left* (Mauro Fermariello), 19 *top centre* and 22 *centre* (Adam Hart-Davis), 23 *centre* and 23 *bottom* (Dr Jeremy Burgess), 30 *bottom left* (David Leah), 36 *top* (Tek Image), 38 *bottom* (Andrew Lambert), 46 *top* (Martyn F Chillmaid), 53 *bottom right* (Brian Brake), 55 *bottom right* (European Space Agency), 64 *top right* and 64 *bottom* (Eckhard Slawik), 64 *centre* (John Sanford), 67 *top* and 67 *centre right* (Andrew Syred), 65 and 69 *left* (NASA); towhee@westol.com, p25 *centre*. Wellcome Trust Photolibrary pp7 *bottom*, 9 *top*, 13 *bottom*, 6 *top*; www.wvminesafety.org/canary.jpg p 39 *top*.

Cover photographs by: Science Photo Library/Tom van Sany (satellite view of the Earth); Science Photo Library/William Ervin (keel-billed toucan); Science Photo Library/Matthew Oldfield (parachutist descending – sunset); Science Photo Library/Simon Fraser (icebergs and penguins, Biscoe Islands, Antartic); Science Photo Library/Dr Jeremy Burgess (background: water droplets).

Project management: Jim Newall
Picture research: Val Mulcahy

Contents

5Aa Food for thought

What is a balanced diet?

Many people love chocolate. This photograph shows a factory where chocolate is made.

> The biggest chocolate bar ever was made in Italy in 2000. It has a mass of over 2 tonnes!

If you only ate chocolate you would not be very healthy. You need to eat different types of food to stay healthy.

You need different sorts of food for:

- energy
- growth
- health.

Mel has made a shopping list.

1 a Write down all the foods on the list.
  b Mel wants to buy a friend's favourite food. What would you want Mel to buy you?

Food for energy

This photograph shows foods that give you energy. Butter and cooking oil contain **fat**. Jam, bread and pasta contain **carbohydrates**. Sweet things contain lots of a carbohydrate called **sugar**. Bread and pasta contain a different carbohydrate called **starch**.

2 a Write down a list of things you have done today which needed energy.
  b What foods have you eaten today to give you energy?

3 Look at Mel's shopping list again. Draw a table to show which foods contain a lot of fat, sugar and starch.

Food for growth

The foods in this photograph will help you to grow. They contain **proteins** which are used to make muscles.

4 What might happen if you did not eat enough protein?

Food for health

Fruits and vegetables contain **fibre** which keeps your insides healthy. They also contain **vitamins** and **minerals** which keep your body working properly. Some other foods also contain vitamins and minerals. **Calcium** is a mineral that helps to make bones and teeth and can be found in milk.

5 Look at Mel's shopping list. Write down foods that are needed for:
a growth **b** health.

Diets

The word **diet** means what you eat. If you eat foods from the different **food groups** (carbohydrates, fats, proteins, vitamins and minerals, fibre) you will have a **balanced diet**.

Food labels

Labels on foods tell you what is in them. This label from a cereal packet tells you that it contains lots of carbohydrate.

	Per 40 g serving	Per 100 g
Energy	540 kJ/ 129 kcal	1350 kJ/ 323 kcal
Protein	4.1 g	10.3 g
Carbohydrate (of which sugars)	25.4 g (7.8 g)	63.5 g (19.5 g)
Fat (of which saturates)	3.5 g (0.8 g)	8.8 g (2.0 g)
Fibre	2.9 g	7.3 g

6 **a** Name a mineral.
b What is this mineral used for?

7 Here is a lunch box.

a Which food groups are missing?
b What would you add to this lunch box to provide these missing food groups?

You should know...

- What a balanced diet is.
- Which foods are needed for energy, for growth and for health.

5Aa Scurvy

How was the cause of scurvy discovered?

Scurvy is a disease that makes your legs swell up, your gums bleed and your teeth fall out. In the 18th century, many sailors got scurvy but no one knew why.

In the middle of the 18th century one sailor was so sick with scurvy that he was left behind on an island. He started to eat grass to keep himself alive, and he got better!

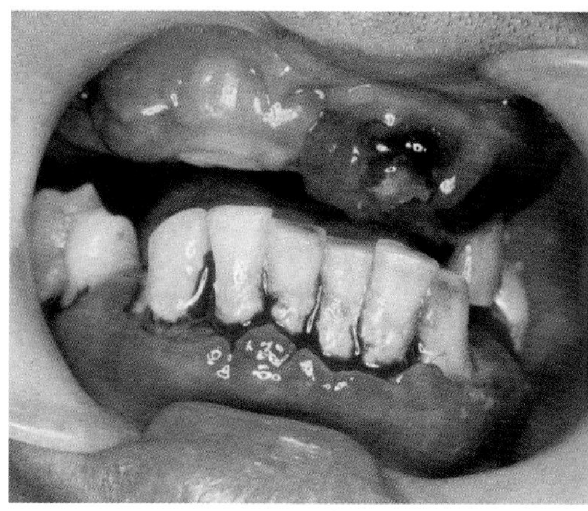

A person with scurvy.

?

1 What happens to you if you get scurvy?

A doctor called James Lind (1716–1794) heard about the sailor. He came up with a **theory** that scurvy was caused by something missing from the sailors' diets. (A theory is a scientific idea that can be tested.) He took some sailors with scurvy and gave them extra parts to their diets, as shown in the table.

Treatment	Extra things added to the diet each day
1	drink cider
2	drink mild acid
3	drink vinegar
4	drink salty water
5	eat an orange and a lemon
6	drink barley water

The sailors who ate fruit got better! Limes worked particularly well so from 1795 all sailors in the British Navy were given lime juice to drink. Scurvy was no longer a problem and British sailors got the nickname of 'limeys'.

Limes helped to keep sailors healthy on long voyages.

?

2 a What was James Lind's idea about how scurvy was caused?
  b What gave him this idea?
  c How did he test his idea?

3 We now know that scurvy is caused by a lack of a vitamin. Find out which vitamin.

You should know...

- What a theory is.

5Ab Healthy exercises

What happens when we exercise?

Proteins in your diet are very important for making muscles. A mineral called calcium is important for making bones. To keep your muscles and bones strong and healthy you also need to exercise.

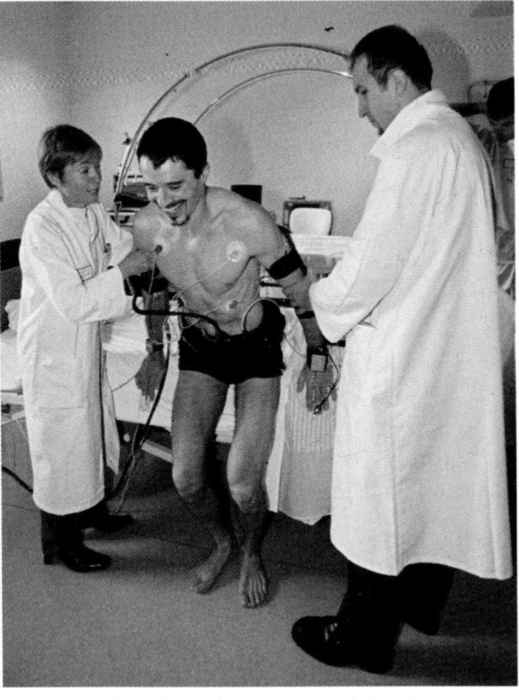

This man has been lying in bed for four months, as part of an experiment. He cannot walk on his own because his muscles have become so weak.

?

1 What food group is needed for:
 a muscles
 b bones?
2 This person has had a broken leg. He has just had the plaster cast removed. Which leg do you think had the plaster cast on it? Explain why you think that.

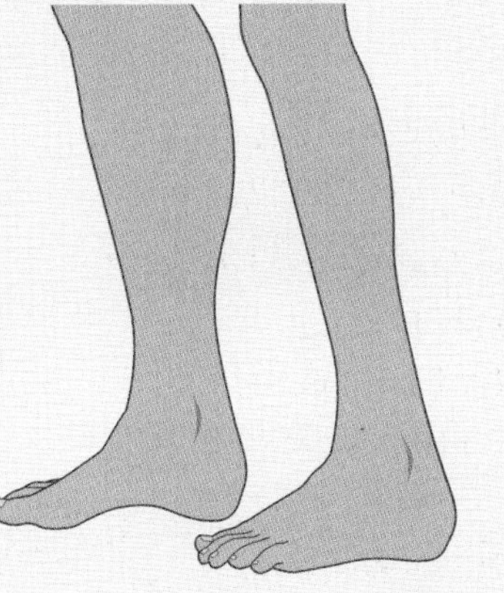

When you move, you use muscles to move your bones. When you do exercise your muscles have to work harder.

?

3 a When you do hard exercise, your muscles may ache. Why?
 b Write down some other ways your body changes when you do exercise.
 c What happens after you have stopped exercising?
4 You need energy for your muscles to move. Name a food group that can supply energy.

You should know...

- What muscles do.
- The effects of exercise on the body.

5Ab Where the heart is

Where is the heart and what does it do?

When you do hard exercise you can often feel your **heart** thumping. Your heart is an **organ** made mainly of muscle. An organ is a part of the body that has a very important job. Your heart is so important that it is well protected by bones called **ribs**.

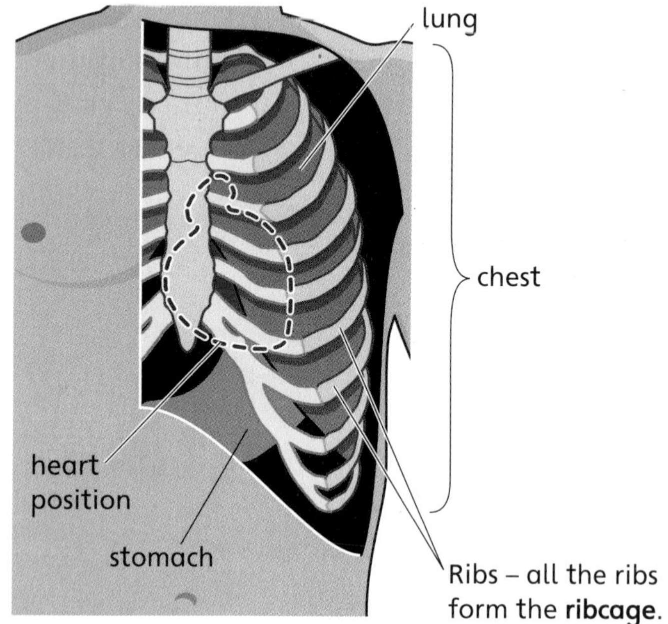

1 Copy and complete these sentences.
   a The heart is an ______ which is protected by ______ called ribs.
   b All the ribs together are called the ______.

Pumps

The photographs show a pump being used. You squash the pump with your hand and let go. Doing this over and over again moves the liquid.

Your heart pumps blood and works in a similar way. It squashes up (**contracts**) and then gets bigger again. It keeps on doing this and so pumps blood around your body.

William Harvey (1578–1678) was the first person to show that the heart was a pump.

2 Describe how the heart moves as it pumps blood.

The photograph shows a heart. The drawing shows what it looks like inside.

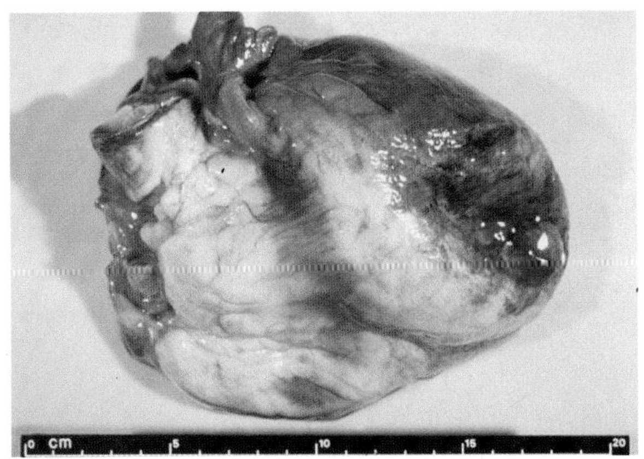

Your heart is about the same size as your clenched fist.

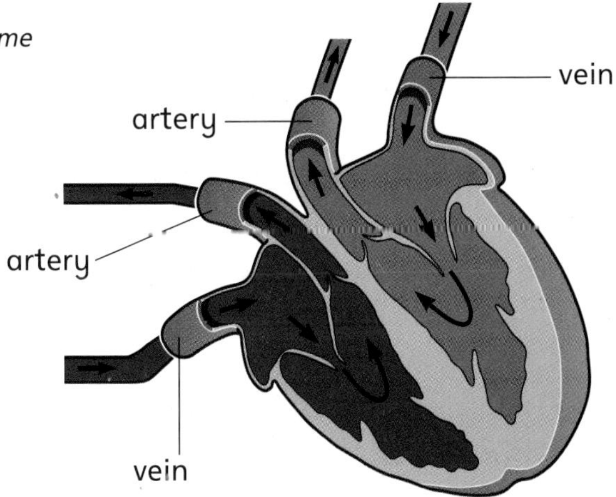

Your heart pumps about 3 litres of blood every minute.

Each time the heart contracts and gets bigger again is called a **heartbeat**. When the heart contracts it squeezes blood out into tubes called **arteries**. When the heart gets bigger again, it fills with blood from other tubes called **veins**. All tubes that carry blood are called **blood vessels**.

3 What does the word 'contract' mean?

4 Which of these are blood vessels?

artery	chest	lung
muscle	stomach	vein

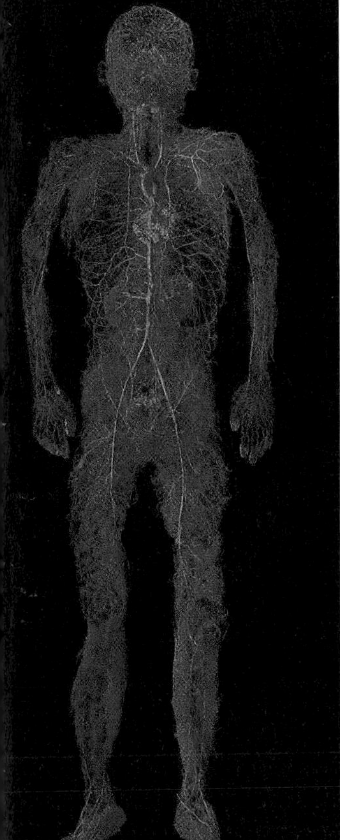

Round and round

Blood carries food and oxygen, which are needed by all the parts of your body. The food comes from what you eat and the oxygen comes from the air you breathe. Your heart pumps blood through millions of blood vessels to make sure that every part of your body gets enough food and oxygen. The picture shows the blood vessels inside your **circulatory system**.

5 Why does your heart need to pump blood?

6 What is the difference between an artery and a vein?

7 Look at the pump on the opposite page. How is this pump different from the heart? List as many differences as you can.

You should know...

- The heart is protected by ribs.
- The heart muscle contracts to pump blood around the body.
- What veins and arteries are.

Heartbeat

What is your pulse rate and how do you measure it?

Doctors can hear your heart beating with a stethoscope. They can count how many times your heart beats in a minute.

The stethoscope was invented in 1816 by René Laënnec (1781–1826). His first one was made of 24 pieces of paper rolled up into a tube!

Another way of finding out how many times your heart beats in a minute is to measure your **pulse**. You can feel your pulse on your wrist. What you feel is your blood being pushed through your arteries with each heartbeat. Your **pulse rate** is the number of times you can feel your pulse in one minute. It is measured in **beats per minute**.

P

How would you measure your pulse rate?

- How many measurements will you make? Why?

?

1 Why do you have a pulse?

2 Eric measured his pulse rate four times in a row.

Try	Result (beats per minute)
1	88
2	86
3	89
4	45

a Why do you think that his results are not all the same?

b Which do you think is the least accurate result?

c Explain your answer to part **b**.

You should know...

- What your pulse rate is and how to measure it.

5Ac Investigating pulse rates

Does exercise affect your pulse rate?

P

How can you find out what affects your pulse rate?

- The things that can be changed when you do an experiment are called **factors**. Which factor will you investigate to find out its effect on your pulse rate?
- How will you change this factor?
- In a **fair test** you can only change one factor at a time. What other factors will you need to keep the same? How will you do this?
- What do you think will happen? This is your **prediction**. Why do you think this will happen?
- Where can you do your investigation safely?
- What apparatus will you need?
- How many measurements will you take? Why?

I think that if you run your pulse rate goes up, but if you run on the spot it does not change. So only the type of exercise you do affects your pulse rate.

When I do hard exercise, I sometimes feel a throbbing in my neck. I think that the harder the exercise you do, the more your pulse rate goes up.

I think your pulse rate goes up when you do exercise.

When I exercise, I can feel my heart. I don't think exercise changes your pulse rate, only how hard your heart beats.

I think that the longer you exercise, the more your pulse rate goes up.

5Ac Changing pulse rates

When does your pulse rate go up?

This person is wearing a pulse rate monitor. It measures her pulse rate electronically. She is taking part in a game show where she has to get across a tightrope without her pulse rate going above a certain level.

When you are nervous your pulse rate goes up. After you stop being nervous your pulse rate comes back down.

Your pulse rate also goes up when you exercise. This is good for you since it gives your heart some exercise and keeps it fit! The harder the exercise you do, the more your pulse rate goes up, until it reaches a maximum.

Your pulse rate will go back to normal after you have stopped being nervous or finished doing exercise. This takes some time to happen but it takes less time if:

- you have been nervous, rather than doing exercise
- your exercise was not very hard.

?

1 Put these three people in order of pulse rate. Write down the person with the highest pulse rate first.

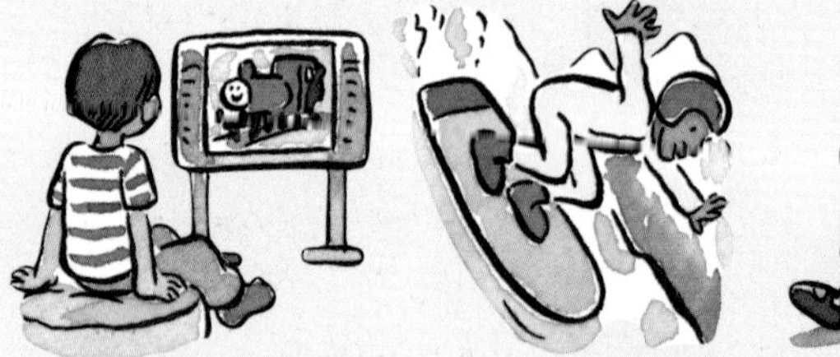

Ben. *Owen.* *Rachel.*

2 These three people have higher pulse rates than normal.
   a Whose pulse rate will take the longest to go back to normal?
   b Explain your answer to part **a**.

Harry. *Dina.* *Megan.*

You should know...

- Your pulse rate takes time to go back to normal after exercise.

5Ac Focus on: Heart bypass surgery

What is heart bypass surgery?

A healthy heart lives in a healthy body

Get moving

Be smoke free

Healthy eating

Remember, nobody can take better care of your heart than you

People who lead unhealthy lives have a higher risk of getting problems with their hearts. Eating too many fatty foods, not taking exercise, drinking too much alcohol and smoking are all bad for your heart.

Blood vessels called **coronary arteries** bring blood to your heart muscle. If you eat too much fat, some of it can stick to the insides of these arteries and block them. This means that not enough blood can get to the heart muscle, so it does not get enough food and oxygen. Parts of the heart can start to die.

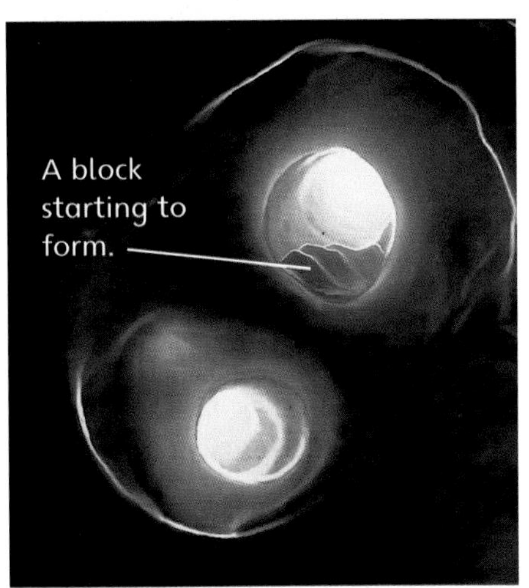

A person with a blocked coronary artery may need a **heart bypass operation**. A piece of vein is cut out of the person (from the leg, for example) and sewn into the artery either side of the blockage. The blood can now go around the blockage.

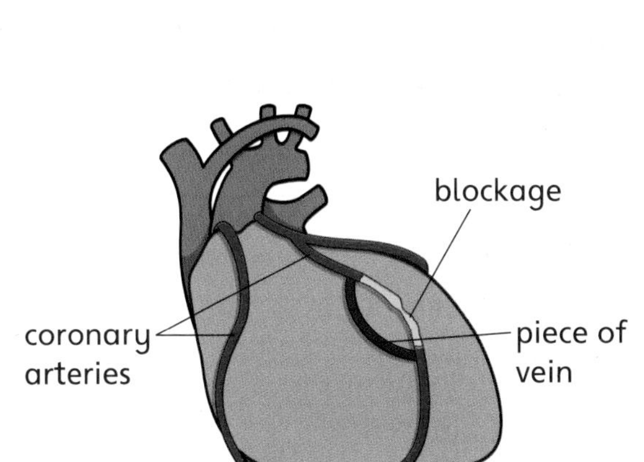

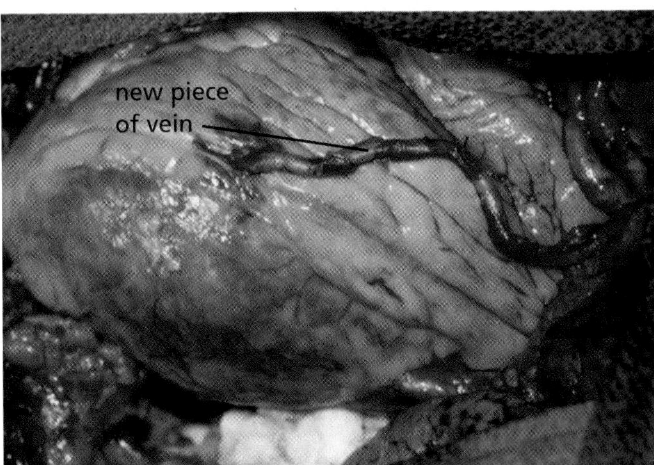

This heart has a new piece of vein sewn into it.

?

1 a Which arteries supply the heart muscle with blood?
  b How can these become blocked?
2 Why does the heart muscle need to be supplied with blood?
3 **Heart disease** is when a small part of the heart has started to die. The heart will not pump so hard. What activities do you think a person with heart disease cannot do? Explain your answer.

5Ad On the pulse

Why does your pulse rate go up when you exercise?

When scientists are measuring things to answer a question, they usually repeat their measurements to make sure they have not made a mistake.

They also take measurements from many different people to check that all their results follow a similar pattern. For example, a scientist may make a prediction that all pupils in Year 5 have the same pulse rate. If only one person's pulse rate was measured, the scientist could not say if the prediction was right or wrong.

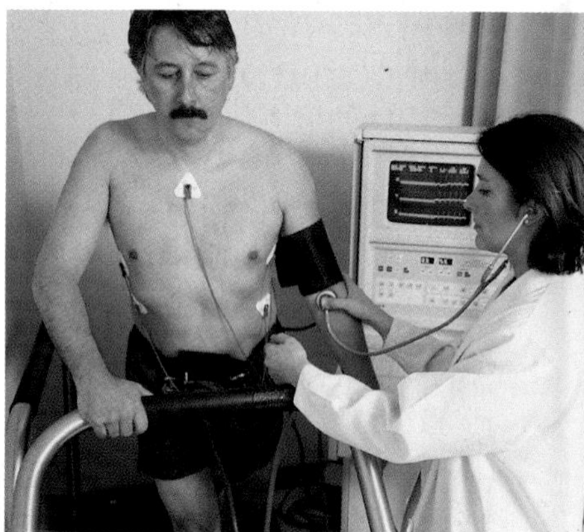

This scientist is investigating how exercise changes the pulse rate.

1 A scientist wants to test the prediction that people's pulse rates never go above 140 beats per minute. Why should the scientist measure the pulse rates of more than one person?

Scientists show their measurements in tables and graphs.
These tables show some measurements of pulse rates after exercise.

Time after exercise (minutes)	Pulse rate (beats per minute)
0	130
2	104
4	88
6	88
8	88

Anita's results.

Time after exercise (minutes)	Pulse rate (beats per minute)
0	145
2	115
4	96
6	86
8	86

Bethany's results.

The scientist wants to draw a **line graph**.

- Which of these shows a line graph of Anita's pulse rate?

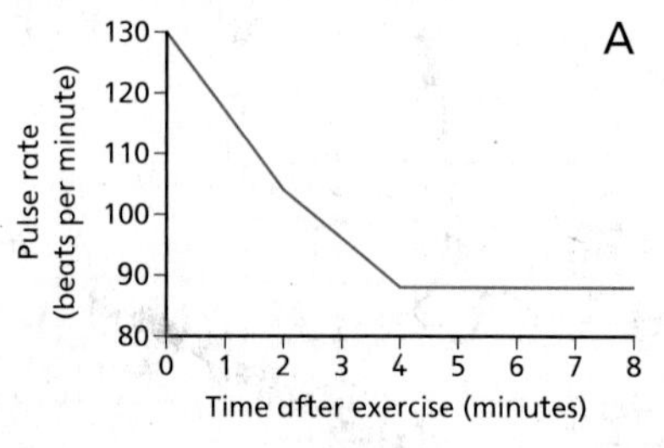

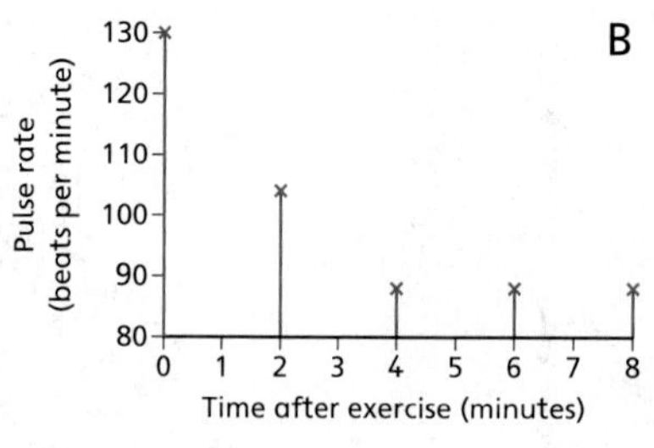

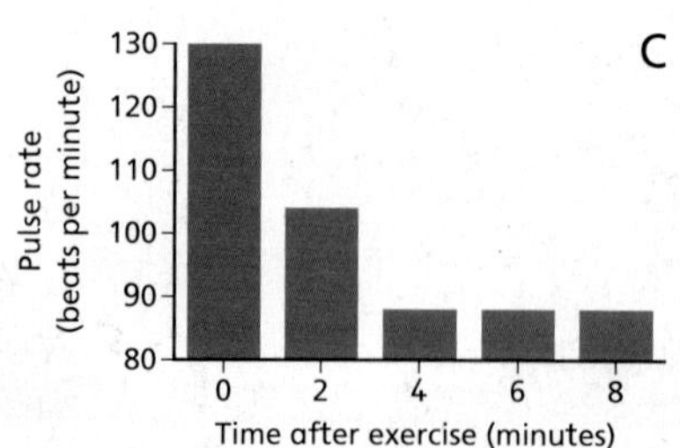

- Which person was doing the harder exercise? Explain your answer.

Muscles and exercise

On the right of this photograph you can see muscles.

Muscles are attached to **bones** and move them at your **joints**. Your elbow is a joint. In your elbow, muscles in your upper arm move bones in your lower arm. Muscles come in pairs. One muscle in the pair pulls a bone one way, and the other muscle pulls the bone the other way.

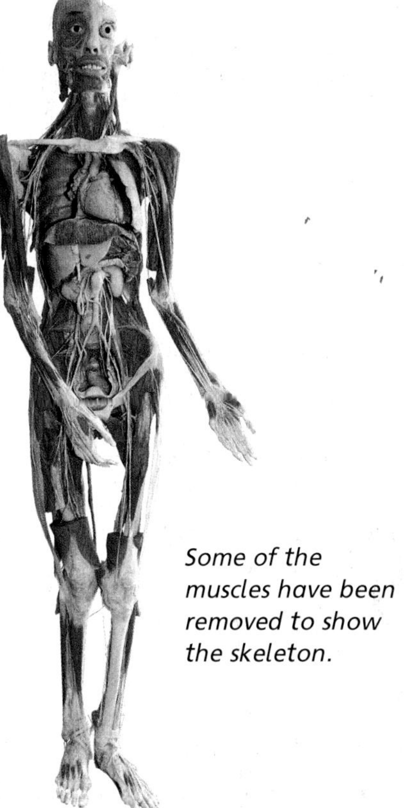

Some of the muscles have been removed to show the skeleton.

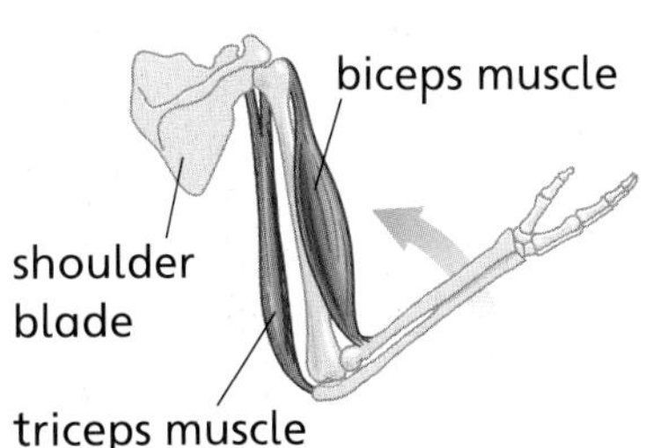

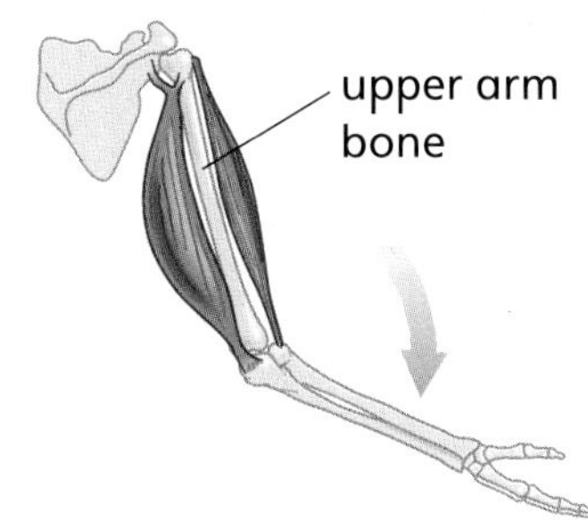

Your **biceps** muscle **contracts** (gets shorter) when you move your lower arm up. Your **triceps** muscle **relaxes** (gets longer). To move your arm back down, your triceps muscle contracts and your biceps muscle relaxes.

When you exercise your muscles have to contract and relax more often. More blood is needed by the muscles and so your heart beats faster.

?

2 What moves the bones in your skeleton?

3 What is the scientific word used when a muscle:
   a gets shorter
   b gets longer again?

4 Name two joints.

5 For each of these people, write down where the muscles are that have caused their hearts to beat faster.
   a A man doing push-ups.
   b A woman running.
   c A boy swimming.

?

6 This graph shows Sasha's pulse rate during two and a half hours. Write down which letter on the graph shows when Sasha was:
   a at a power aerobics class
   b having something to eat
   c jogging for the bus.

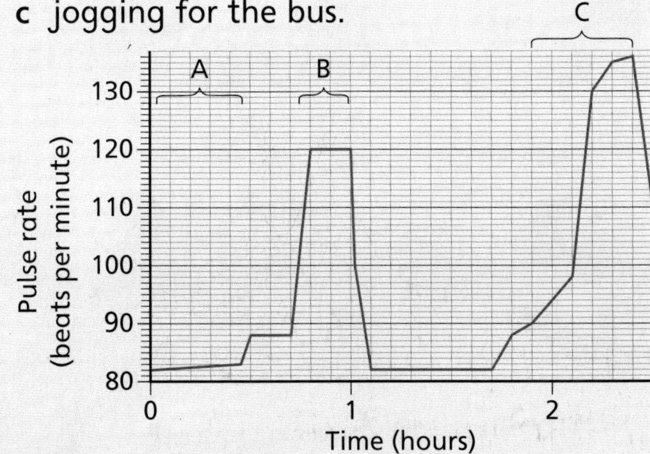

Sasha's pulse rate changed as she did different things.

You should know...

- Why scientists take lots of measurements.
- What a line graph is.
- Why your heart beats faster when you exercise.

5Ae Drugs

What are the dangers of some drugs?

In 1999 Maurice Green broke the world record for the 100 metres, with a time of 9.79 seconds. However, back in 1988 Ben Johnson had already run the 100 metres in 9.79 seconds and won an Olympic gold medal for it! Two days after Johnson won this medal, it was taken away from him because he was found to have used **drugs** to help him win.

Maurice Green broke the 100 metres record fairly.

Medicines

A drug is a substance that changes the way your body works. Some drugs are useful. **Medicines** are drugs that can help us recover from illnesses. These include things like aspirin and antibiotics.

Many drugs can only be bought if you have been to see a doctor. This is because many medicines are dangerous if:

- they are taken by people who are allergic to them
- too much is taken
- they have **side-effects**.

A side-effect is an unpleasant effect caused by a medicine. Side-effects include things like headaches or feeling sick.

?

1 a What is a drug?
  b Give two examples.

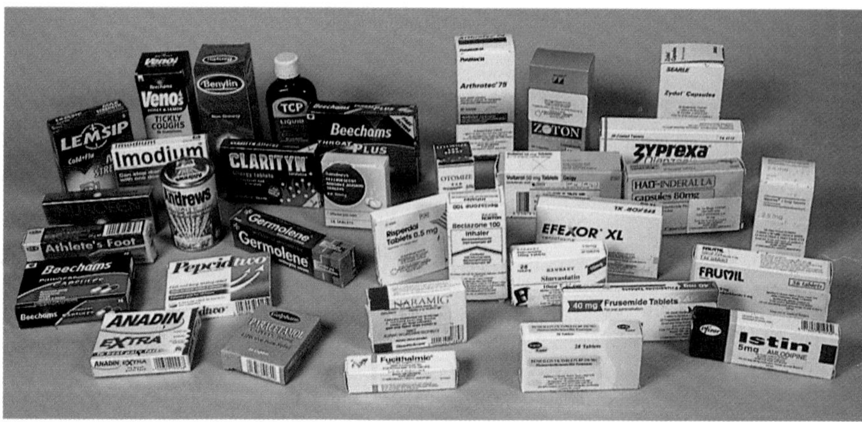

You can buy some of these medicines only if your doctor says so.

?

2 What is a side-effect?
3 Look at the photograph of the medicines. Which side of the photograph shows medicines you can buy in the shops?
4 Why should you always take medicines exactly as the instructions say on the packet?

Cigarettes

People smoke to take in a drug called **nicotine**. This drug makes people feel more relaxed. However, it is **addictive**, which means that people feel that they cannot cope without it. Nicotine can cause arteries to get blocked up which can cause **heart attacks** (when the heart stops working). Smoke also contains a sticky black substance called **tar** which can cause **lung cancer** and breathing problems.

a smoker

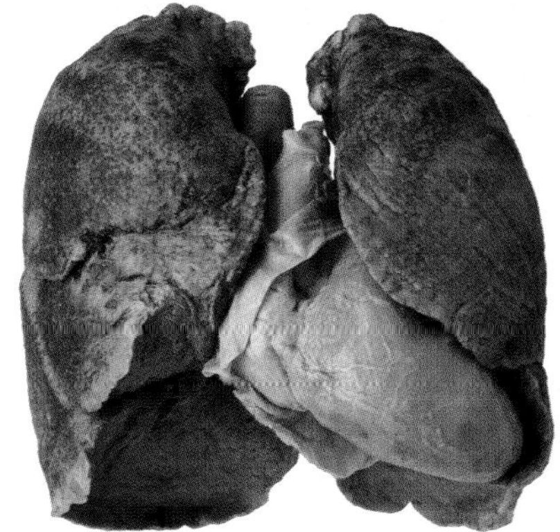

a non-smoker

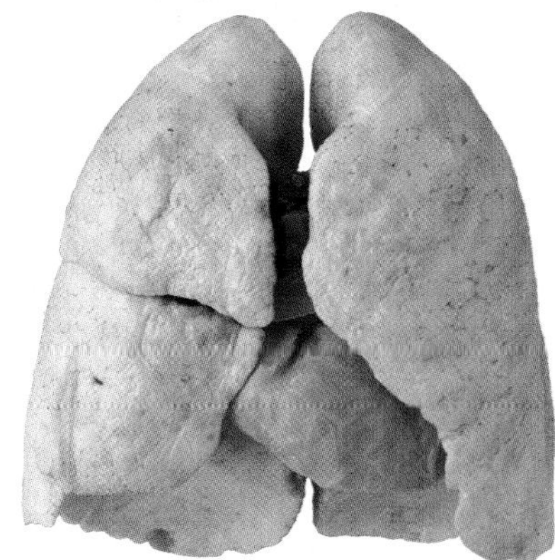

Tar collects in the lungs of smokers.

5 List some problems caused by smoking.
6 People called alcoholics are addicted to alcohol. What does this mean?

Alcohol

Alcohol is not too bad for you in small amounts. In large quantities it damages your stomach, your liver and your brain.

Illegal drugs

Many drugs are banned completely because they are extremely dangerous. We say they are **illegal**. They include things like heroin and cocaine. Most illegal drugs are addictive and can cause brain damage and death.

Solvent abuse

Sniffing the fumes given off by some strong glues and lighter fluid is also addictive and causes serious brain damage. Sniffing glues is known as **solvent abuse**.

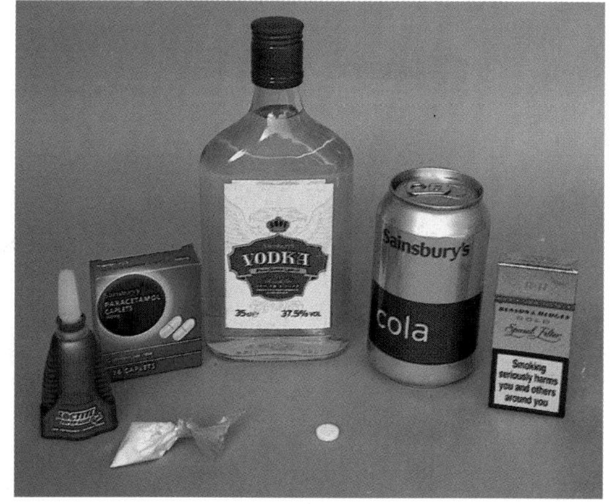

Some drugs.

7 Look at the photograph of drugs.
  a Which of them are you allowed to buy now?
  b Which of them can only be bought by adults?
8 Name two illegal drugs. Say why you think they are illegal.

You should know...

- Drugs change the way your body works.
- Some drugs are addictive.
- The problems caused by smoking, drinking alcohol and taking some medicines and illegal drugs.

5Ba Mixed fruits

Why do plants have fruits?

Many plants make **fruits**. Fruits come in many shapes and sizes. Here are just a few.

Tomatoes are fruits!

The fruit pods on this Cacao *tree are where chocolate comes from.*

> **?**
> **1** What is odd about where the *Cacao* tree fruits are?

Plants that have flowers are called **flowering plants**. The flowers produce fruits which contain **seeds**. Not all flowering plants have brightly coloured flowers. Grass and wheat are flowering plants!

Wheat flowers.

Wheat fruits. Each one contains a seed.

Some fruits are juicy and some are dry. For example, oranges are juicy but grass fruits are dry.

> **?**
> **2** What do fruits contain?
> **3** Name two fruits which are:
> **a** juicy
> **b** dry.

The seeds inside fruits can grow into new plants. Plants use seeds to **reproduce**.

Fruits are used to move seeds from the plant where they were made to a new place, so that the young plant can grow in a new area. This is called **seed dispersal**.

Fruits are food for many animals, including humans, and this helps to disperse the seeds. Seeds are also dispersed by wind, water and explosions and by attaching themselves to animals.

A Swiss scientist, George De Mestral (1907–1990), invented Velcro™ by examining how fruits with hooks stuck to his clothes!

Coconuts are spread by water.

Dandelion fruits are spread by the wind.

This bird dropping contains seeds from the fruit that the bird has eaten.

These lupin fruits explode, throwing out the seeds.

These burdock fruits have hooks which catch on animal fur, so they get carried away by the animals.

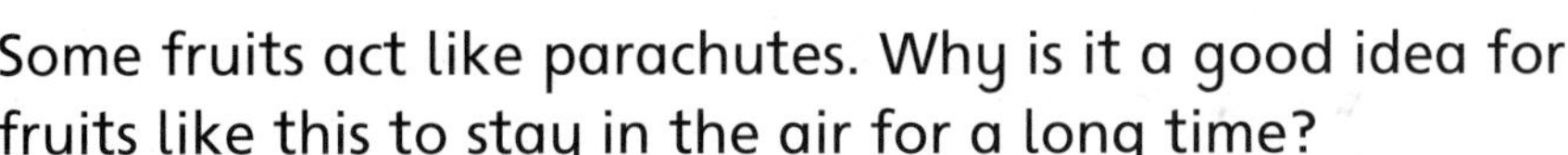

Some fruits act like parachutes. Why is it a good idea for fruits like this to stay in the air for a long time?

- Which of these parachutes do you think will stay in the air longer?
- How could you check to see if you are right?

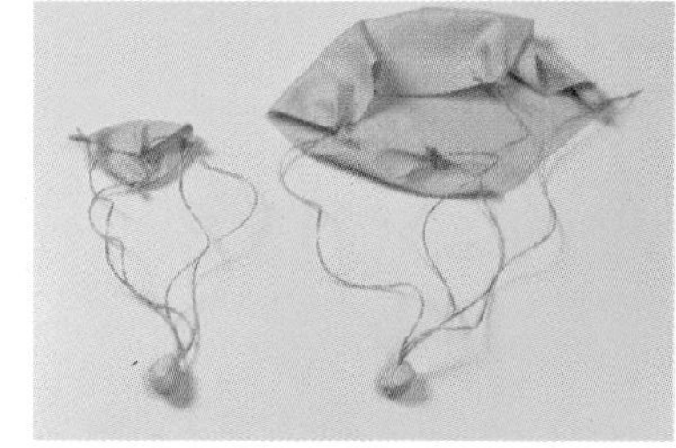

As well as helping plants spread to a new area, seed dispersal helps to make sure that the new plants have a good chance of surviving. If seeds start to grow right underneath a parent plant, the new plants may not get enough water and light to grow properly. The bigger plant uses up the water and its leaves block out the light.

You should know...

- How and why seeds are dispersed.
- Flowers are needed for reproduction.

4 Why do plants have fruits?

5 a Why do seeds need to be dispersed?

b How can seeds be dispersed?

6 This is the fruit of the sausage tree which grows in Africa. It is a favourite food of hippopotamuses. Explain how this tree disperses its seeds.

Investigating germination

What is needed for germination?

The trees in this forest all grew from seeds. The forest covers a large area because the fruits of the trees have been dispersed.

Once the seeds have been dispersed they need to grow. When a seed starts to grow it is called **germination**. Not all seeds will grow because they need certain things to be able to germinate.

P

How can you find out what affects germination?

- What factors do you think will affect seed germination?
- Which factor will you investigate?
- How will you change this factor?
- How will you make your investigation fair?
- Where will you keep your seeds?
- What apparatus will you need?
- How many seeds will you use? Why?
- When will you check your seeds?
- How will you know when they have germinated?

5Bb Growing from seed

What do seeds need to germinate?

When seeds are dispersed, some will end up in a place where they can't germinate and some will be eaten. This is why plants need to make so many fruits and seeds.

Seeds only germinate when they have the things they need. Seeds that are buried in the ground over the winter will not germinate until it is warmer in the spring. In deserts, seeds will not germinate until it rains. Seeds do *not* need light or soil to germinate.

1 What is germination?
2 Peas are seeds found inside pods.
  a Copy and complete this sentence. A pod is a type of f_______.
  b When the pod dries out, it bursts and throws out the peas. In the drawings, the peas have landed in different places. Which peas will germinate?
  c Explain your answer to part **b**.

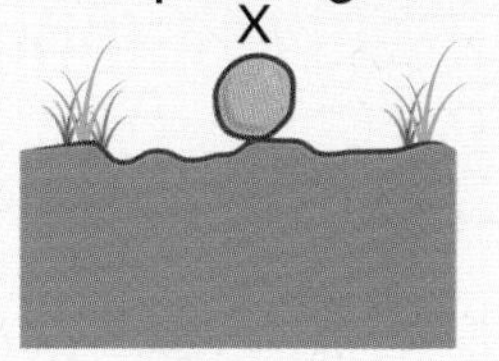

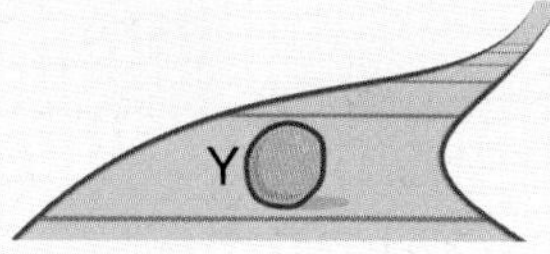

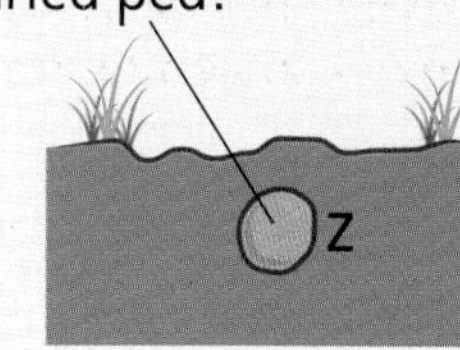

A dry desert.

The same desert after it rained!

The seeds of *Protea* bushes will only germinate once they have been burnt.

3 Name two things that are:
  a needed for germination
  b *not* needed for germination.
4 Seeds are sold in packets. Why don't they germinate in the packets?
5 Why don't oak tree acorns germinate in the winter?

You should know...

- What germination is.
- What things are needed and not needed for germination.

5Bc Making seeds

How do plants make seeds?

When a seed germinates, new roots and shoots grow. Once the little plant has leaves it is called a **seedling**. It now needs light and substances found in the soil called **nutrients**. It still needs water and warmth.

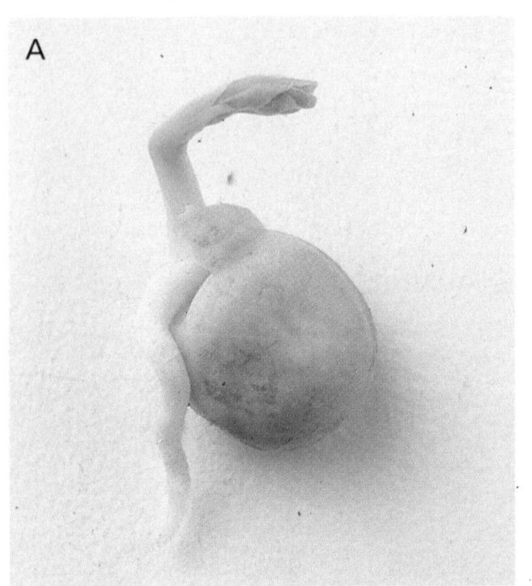

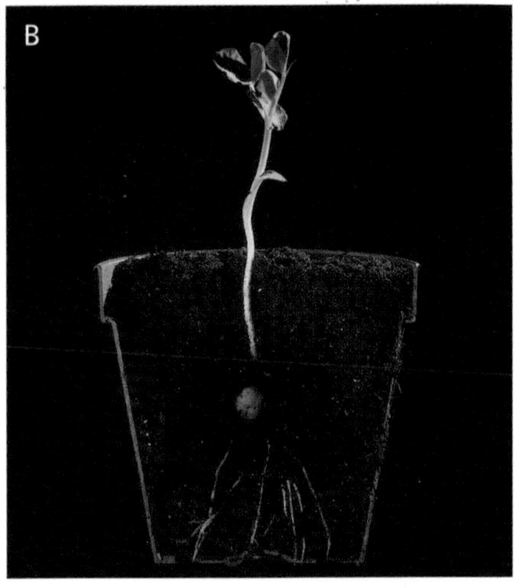

If the plant gets all the things that it needs, it will grow and have flowers. Flowers contain male and female parts (male and female **organs**).

Prospero Alpino (1553–1616) first discovered that flowers had male and female parts.

1 Photographs A, B and C don't have any writing underneath (captions) to say what they show. What captions would you write for these photographs?

2 a What is the male organ of a flower called?
  b List its parts.
  c What does each part do?

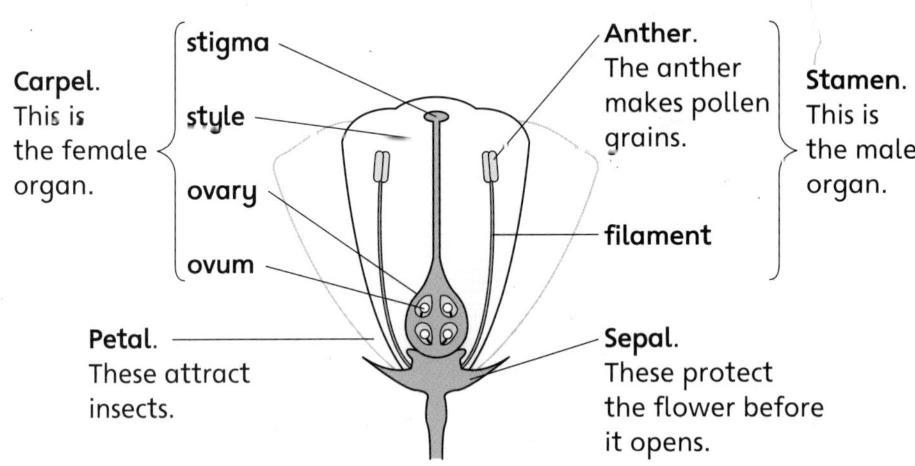

Pollination

To make a seed, **pollen grains** from the male part need to be taken to the **stigma** of another flower. This is called **pollination**.

Insects often pollinate flowers. They are attracted to the flowers by brightly coloured petals, a nice smell and sticky **nectar** which they like to eat. The pollen gets stuck to the insects. When the insects visit other flowers, the pollen is brushed onto the stigmas.

A beetle covered with pollen.

The pollen of some plants is carried by the wind. It is very fine and light so that it can float on the wind. Pollen in the air can cause hay fever.

3 Some plants have flowers in the spring when there are very few insects. How do you think pollination happens in these plants?
4 How do flowers attract insects?
5 Here are two different sorts of pollen magnified 150 times.
   a Which one do you think is carried by the wind? Explain your answer.
   b Why do you think pollen X has spikes on it?

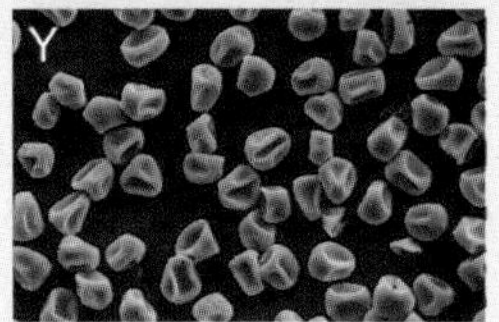

Fertilisation

When a pollen grain lands on a stigma it grows a **pollen tube** which goes down the **style** and into the **ovary**.

Here it reaches an **ovum** (sometimes called an egg). A part of the pollen grain joins with the ovum. This is called **fertilisation**. The fertilised ovum grows into a seed and the ovary can turn into a fruit.

Pollen grains come in different shapes and sizes to make sure that only pollen of the right sort can fertilise an ovum.

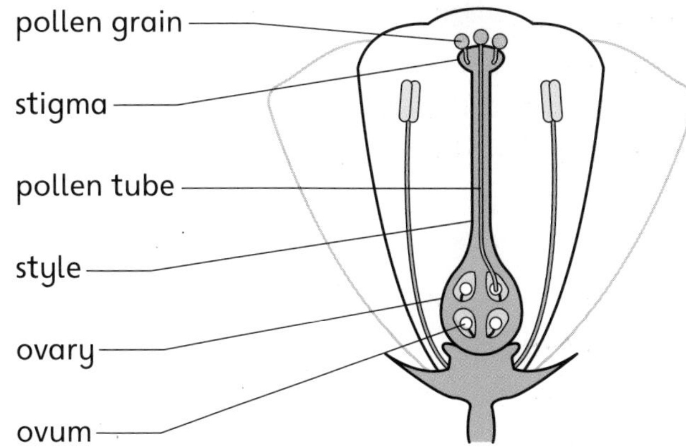

A pollen tube growing.

6 What happens in:
   a pollination
   b fertilisation?
7 Why are pollen grains different shapes and sizes? Give two reasons.
8 Why do you think grass flowers are not brightly coloured?

You should know…

- The parts of the flower and what they do.
- What pollination and fertilisation are.

Plant life cycles

What is a life cycle?

After fertilisation, the fertilised ova grow into seeds. (Ova is the plural of ovum!) The ovary grows into a fruit.

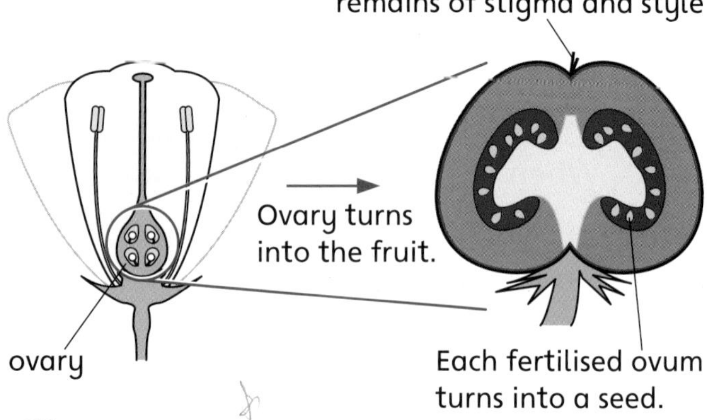

1 What does the ovary from a flower grow into?
2 Look at this fruit. What are the parts labelled A and B?

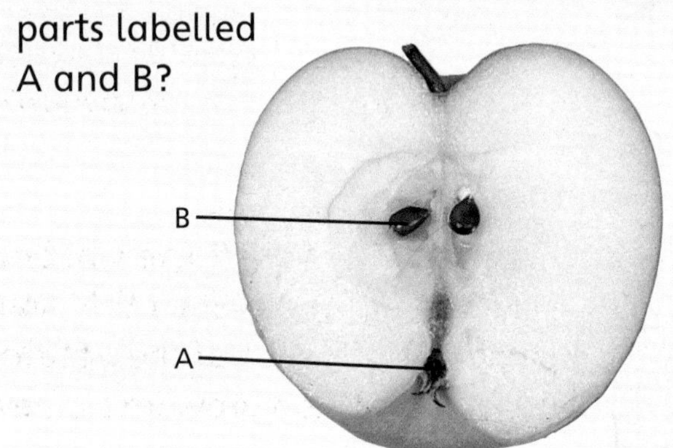

The stages in a plant's life are its **life cycle**. The life cycle shows you what happens from when the plant germinates until it makes its own seeds.

! If you remove the hard part at the end of an orange you will see some small dots inside. The number of dots is the number of slices inside! The dots are the remains of tubes carrying water to the growing slices.

You should know...

- How fruits are formed.
- What a life cycle is.

?

3 a Copy out the diagram below. Write these words in the boxes to show the life cycle of a plant.

fertilisation	germination
makes flowers	pollination

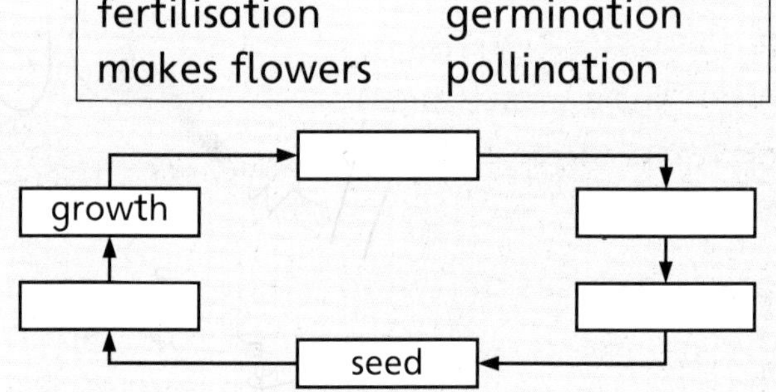

b Why do you think it is called a life *cycle*?

4 Plants need to disperse (spread) both pollen and seeds. Copy out these tables and fill in the gaps. Some have been done for you.

Pollen dispersed by ...	**Example**
insects	foxglove plant
wind	

Seeds dispersed by ...	**Example**
animals eating	
hooks onto animals	

5Bd Focus on: Seedless reproduction

How else can new plants be formed?

Many plants produce seeds that grow into new plants. But some plants have other ways of making new plants. Strawberry plants have flowers that produce fruits but they also grow **runners**. These are little shoots that come out of the plant and grow along the soil. New plants grow out of the runners.

A strawberry plant.

The walking fern has a similar trick. Where the tip of a leaf meets the ground, a new plant can grow!

A walking fern.

Potato plants have flowers but also produce potatoes. When the main plant dies off, each of the potatoes underground can grow into a new plant the following year.

When plants produce seeds, both a male part (pollen grain) and a female part (ovum) are needed. These usually come from two different plants. When plants produce new plants without using seeds, only one plant is needed.

1 What is a strawberry runner?
2 Why do you think the walking fern got its name?
3 Reproducing using only one parent is quicker than making seeds. Why do you think this is?
4 Draw a life cycle diagram for a potato plant. Include both types of reproduction on it.
5 Find out how quaking aspen trees reproduce.

5Be Animal life cycles

What are the stages of an animal life cycle?

Plants and animals, including humans, need to grow and reproduce. We change as we get older and have different stages in our lives.

1 a Look at the drawings of the stages of life. Write in a list, the letters in order of age. Start with the youngest. Put one of these words next to each letter to say what each drawing shows.

adolescence (teenage) adulthood babyhood childhood old age

b How long do you think each stage lasts?

c Which stage are you in?

All animals reproduce and have young (babies). The young grow up and can then also reproduce. Different animals take different lengths of time before they are old enough to have young.

Animal	Time it takes to be able to reproduce
black rat snake	9 years
harvest mouse	45 days
lion	5 years
salmon fish	2 years
zebra	4 years

?

2 a How long does it take for a lion to be able to have young?

b Which animal in the table takes the longest time?

c Do humans take more or less time than this?

3 Katie says that the larger the animal the longer it takes before it can have young. Is she right?

Looking after newly-born animals

Newly-born animals need different amounts of care.
A newly-born zebra can stand after 6 minutes and run after only 45 minutes.
A newly-born lion has its eyes sealed. The eyes only open after two weeks.

This zebra foal is only 10 minutes old.

This lion cub is a week old.

Looking after the young

Many animals look after their young for a long time. Zebras stay with their mothers for 3 years, for protection. Lions also stay with their mothers for 3 years and during this time they learn how to hunt. Human young can stay with their parents for over 18 years!

These barn owl young are looked after until they can fly and hunt for themselves. This takes about 8 weeks.

?

4 Which needs more looking after, a newly-born zebra or a newly-born lion? Explain your answer.
5 Which are looked after for longer, young lions or young barn owls? Why do you think this is?
6 Use the information on these pages to describe the life cycle of a human.
7 Write down one similarity between the human life cycle and a plant life cycle.
8 Why do you think it is a good thing that zebras can run soon after birth?

You should know...

- Animals have young that will grow up and also have young.
- Human young need looking after for a long time compared with other animals.

5Be Gestation times

What is a gestation time?

Mammals are animals that have hair or fur. Some only have a little hair like a human or a hippopotamus.

The young of mammals grow inside the mothers before being born. Most other animals lay eggs. (The young grow inside the eggs and then hatch.)

It takes time for an animal to be ready to be born or hatch. This time is called the **gestation time** (pronounced *'jess-**tay**-shun'*). In humans it is often called **pregnancy**.

Animal	Gestation time
barn owl	33 days
harvest mouse	19 days
hippopotamus	18 months
human	9 months
lion	3 months
salmon fish	2 months
zebra	1 year

Newly-born puppies.

A chick hatching.

?

1 What is a gestation time?
2 Which animal in the table has the shortest gestation time?
3 Which animal has a gestation time twice that of another animal in the table?
4 Use the information on this page and pages 26–27 to describe the life cycles of:
   a lions
   b zebras.
5 a Which animals in the table are mammals?
   b What can you say about the size of the mammal and its gestation time?

! The animal with the longest gestation time is the Asian elephant. It takes 22 months!

You should know...

- What a gestation time is.

5Be Extinction

Why do some animals become extinct?

All living things get old and eventually die. The table shows how long some animals live.

> **!** The oldest living thing is a bristlecone pine tree in California in the USA. It is over 4700 years old.

Animal	How long it lives
black rat snake	30 years
harvest mouse	18 months
human	70–100 years
lion	30 years
zebra	20 years

If living things did not reproduce they would die out and become **extinct**. Many animals have become extinct because humans hunted them. These include a giant bird from New Zealand, called a moa.

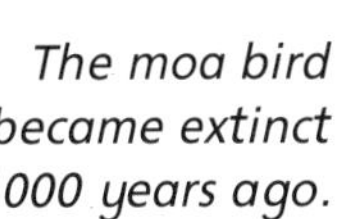

The moa bird became extinct 1000 years ago.

?

1 What would happen if living things did not reproduce?

Some animals are only found in zoos. The last wild barbary lion was shot in 1920 but there are some left in zoos. People are trying to **breed** the ones in zoos and put them back into the wild.

Animals like tigers and red pandas are facing extinction because they are being hunted and their homes are being destroyed. People are trying to save these animals by breeding them in zoos and by trying to protect the areas where they live.

The red panda is facing extinction in the Himalaya mountains due to hunting and the cutting down of the forests where it lives.

?

2 Name one animal that has become extinct.
3 Write down two reasons why animals may become extinct.
4 What can people do to try to stop living things becoming extinct?
5 Find out why the dodo bird became extinct.

You should know...

- Why some living things become extinct.
- What can be done to stop this.

5Ca Solids, liquids and gases

What are the properties of solids, liquids and gases?

When we describe what materials are like, we are describing their **properties**. For instance, one property of ice is that it is hard.

A room in the Ice Hotel in northern Sweden. The whole building is made out of ice, even the furniture!

Solids and liquids

Ice is a **solid**. When ice **melts** it becomes a **liquid**. Solids and liquids have different properties.

1 Here are some pictures of different materials. Draw a table to show which ones are solids and which ones are liquids.

Orange juice.

Pottery.

Engine oil.

Milk.

Paper.

Stone.

2 Here are some properties of solids and liquids.

hard

runny

They don't change shape.

They take the shape of the container they are in.

The amount of space they take up (**volume**) does not change.

a Which are properties of solids?
b Which are properties of liquids?
c Which property is the same for both solids and liquids?
d What does the word 'volume' mean?

Gases

Some things are not solids or liquids; they are **gases**. The air is made of gases. You cannot see air but we know that it is real because many things would not work if air were not made of anything.

This pedal powered aeroplane could not fly if air were not real. It needs air to support its wings.

This boat needs air in its sails. It sailed around the World in just over 64 days and is the current holder of the Jules Verne Trophy.

*The air slows down the parachute. When air slows things down it is called **air resistance**.*

We can often feel air, especially when it is moving. We can feel the wind blowing. This helps us to know that air is a real thing. Something that helps us to know that an idea is right is called **evidence**.

?

3 What do we call moving air?

4 a Which of these illustrations show evidence that air is real?

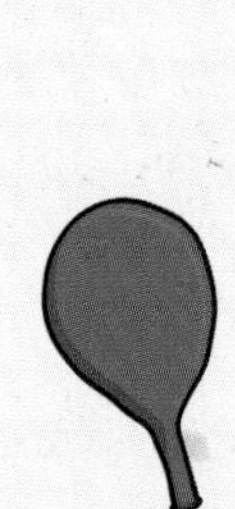

A jar of air.

b Think of another piece of evidence that helps you to know that air is real.

5 What is air resistance?

You should know...

- Some properties of solids and liquids.
- Air is made of gases.
- What evidence is.

5Cb Air is real!

How can we see that air is real?

This is an escape slide from an aeroplane. The slide is stored in the door. If it is needed, it fills with air which makes it stiff enough to let people slide down it. This is another piece of evidence to show that air is a real thing.

1 The escape slide is 'inflatable'. Name two other objects that are inflatable.

This escape slide fills with air in about 5 seconds.

Mass

The **mass** of something is the amount of material it contains. It is often measured in **grams**. We can measure the mass of something using a **balance**. Air is a material and so it has a mass, although only a very small one.

Ash is measuring the masses of two beach balls. He is using a digital balance.

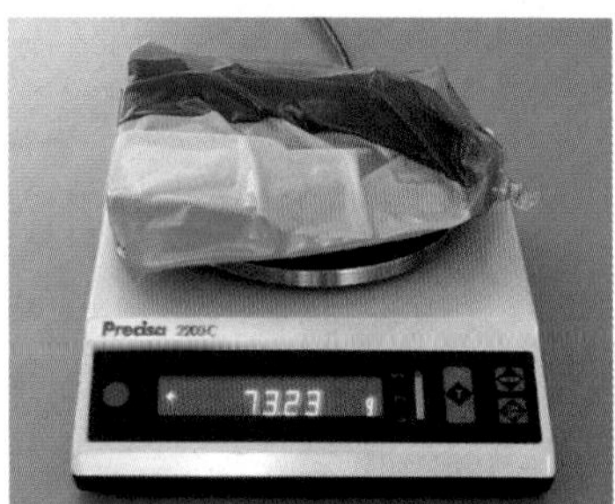

- Which balloon has the biggest mass and why?

1 litre of air has a mass of 1.22 g.
1 litre of water has a mass of 1000 g.

2 What do we use to measure the masses of things?
3 When does an escape slide have the most mass? Is it just before it opens or after it is fully open? Explain your answer.
4 Put the following in order, starting with the one with the least mass.

1 cm^3 of steel
1 cm^3 of air
1 cm^3 of water
1 cm^3 of sponge

This picture shows a sea sponge living under the sea. It is attached to rocks and feeds by sucking water in and out through the holes in its surface. The water contains the things that it eats. Some people use sea sponges instead of plastic ones when they have a bath.

?

5 Do you think sponge is a solid, a liquid or a gas? Explain your choice.

6 What are the sea sponge's holes full of when it is:

a in the sea

b sitting on the side of a bath?

C

Anil held a sponge underwater and squeezed it. In his book he wrote down what he saw (his **observation**).

When I squeezed the sponge I saw bubbles.

- What do you think the bubbles were made of?
- Where did the bubbles come from?
- Anil did not expect to get bubbles! How could he check to see if his observation was right?

You should know...

- Some solids have gaps in or between them that can fill with air.
- You need to repeat observations to be sure of your results.

P

Chelsea has a jar of marbles. She pours water over them.

- What do you **predict** will happen (what will her observation be)?
- Why do you think this will happen?
- What would you do to find out if you are right?

5Cc Investigating air spaces

How could you find out how much air is in different soils?

Many things contain spaces in them that are filled with air. Even soil has air spaces. Animals like worms need air to breathe so the spaces are important. Some soils contain more air spaces than other soils.

Sandy soils have lots of air spaces.

Clay soils do not have many air spaces.

?

1 Why are air spaces important in soil?

2 Would you expect to find more animals in a sandy soil or a clay one? Explain your answer.

P

How would you measure the amount of air in different soils?

- What apparatus will you need?
- How will you use your apparatus and what will you measure?
- Will you need to do any calculations to work out your answer? If so, what calculations will you do?
- How will you check to make sure your measurements are correct?
- How will you make your investigation a fair test?

5Cc Different sorts of gases

How are different gases used?

Soil contains lumps of dirt (**solids**), water (a **liquid**) and air (which is made from **gases**). All these things take up space and so they are called **matter**. Solids, liquids and gases are the three different forms that matter can be in. These are the three **states of matter**.

1 What are the three states of matter?

Soils contain a mixture of different solids. Most soils contain sand and clay, which are both solids. In the same way, the air contains a mixture of different gases. One of the other gases in air is **carbon dioxide**. We use carbon dioxide to make fizzy drinks.

Fizzy drinks contain carbon dioxide.

Fizzy drinks were invented in 1772 by Joseph Priestley (1733–1804).

A tiny amount of the air is a gas called **helium**. We put helium in balloons to make them rise.

A balloon filled with helium.

2 What do we use carbon dioxide for?

3 Lemonade has bubbles in it. What are these bubbles made of?

Another gas in the air is called **oxygen** which animals need to breathe. Oxygen is used in hospitals to help people with breathing problems.

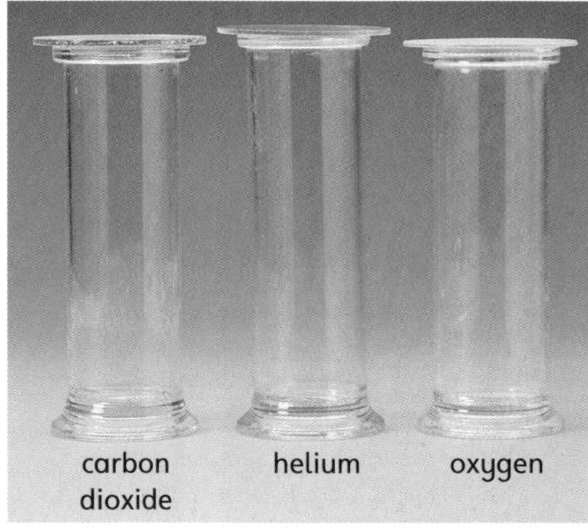

Three different gases.

4 Name two ways in which the gases on this page are similar.

5 Find out how some other gases, including natural gas, are used.

You should know...

- The three states of matter.
- There are different gases which have different uses.

5Cc Focus on: Gases and lighting

How are gases used in lights?

Most of the air is **nitrogen** gas. Just over 100 years ago, scientists found that nitrogen taken from the air was heavier than nitrogen made in other ways. William Ramsay (1852–1916) came up with a **theory** that the nitrogen taken from the air contained other gases that made it heavier. He was right and discovered the gases neon, argon, krypton and xenon (pronounced '***zen**-on*').

These gases are now used for lighting. Light bulbs are filled with **argon**. If oxygen from the air reaches the glowing wire inside a light bulb, the wire breaks. Filling light bulbs with argon stops this happening.

Neon is used in signs which glow. A glass tube is made into the right shape and all the air is sucked out. Then a small amount of neon is put inside. When electricity flows through the gas it glows red. Argon (mixed with a little of a liquid metal called mercury) can be used too, and this gives a blue colour.

Electricity flows through **xenon** in some car headlight bulbs. These bulbs give a much brighter light than normal headlights which have glowing wires inside them.

?

1 What is a theory?
2 Look at the photograph above of the lit-up hotel. What gas is used in:
   a tube A
   b tube B?
3 **a** In the photographs on the left, which car has the xenon-filled headlight bulbs?
   b Explain how you worked out your answer.
4 Find out what krypton is used for.

5Cd Evaporation

What is evaporation?

This photograph of a pond in Shropshire was taken in 1976. It did not rain all summer. Most of the water changed into a gas called **water vapour** leaving only a very small pond. When a liquid changes into gas the process is called **evaporation**.

?

1 What state of matter is the water in the pond?
2 a What will happen to these wet clothes?
  b Why will this happen?
3 What does liquid water form when it evaporates?

Bigger amounts of water take longer to evaporate because more water needs to be turned into water vapour. It only takes a couple of hours for puddles to dry up but it took many months for the pond to dry up.

Lucy did an experiment to see how long it would take for two different volumes of water to evaporate.

The different volumes of water took the same amount of time to evaporate. This was not what she expected. Her teacher said that this is because she did not do a fair test.

- Why was this not a fair test?

You should know...

- When a liquid turns into a gas it is called evaporation.

5Cd Smelly gases

How can we smell liquids?

Different places have different smells. Smells are caused by smelly gases in the air going into your nose. Smelly gases are often from liquids that have evaporated.

Gases spread all over the place. In the picture below, Mr Hamilton is wearing aftershave. Jody will smell the aftershave first. It will take longer for Bill to smell it because it takes extra time for the smelly gas to spread through the air and reach him.

1 Write a list of words that describe smells (e.g. pong).

2 a What do you think the places in photographs A and B smell like?

b Where do you think the smells of these places have come from?

3 Look at the picture of the classroom. Write down the order in which the children will smell Mr Hamilton's aftershave.

This flower gives off a smell of rotting meat to attract flies. The flies pollinate the flower.

You can't see most gases but you can see bromine. Bromine liquid has been added to this container of air. The liquid evaporates and you can see how the brown gas is spreading all around the container. Gases fill the containers they are put in.

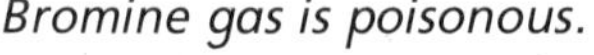

Bromine gas is poisonous.

You should know...

- We can smell some liquids because they evaporate and the vapour spreads through the air.

5Cd Focus on: Detecting gases

How are dangerous gases detected?

Coal mining is a dangerous job. Mines can fill with a poisonous gas called **carbon monoxide**. It has no smell and you can't see it. Before the invention of modern equipment to detect this gas, miners used to take canary birds to work. The birds stopped singing if the amount of carbon monoxide got too much. The miners then knew it was time to leave the mine.

A canary.

A carbon monoxide detector. The circle turns from orange to black if there is too much carbon monoxide.

Natural gas fires and boilers can also produce carbon monoxide if they are not looked after properly. Detectors can show if carbon monoxide is being produced.

Natural gas is also found in mines and can explode. Like carbon monoxide, it is invisible and has no smell. This was a big problem for coal miners before the invention of electric torches. They used to use flames in their lamps which could make the natural gas explode.

> **!** In 1913, 436 miners were killed by a natural gas explosion in a coal mine in Senghenydd, Wales.

Even today, leaks in pipes carrying natural gas can cause explosions. However, natural gas now has a smell added to it so that people can tell if there is a leak.

?

1. Why are these gases dangerous?
   a carbon monoxide
   b natural gas
2. Where in a house might you find both natural gas and carbon monoxide?
3. Why does natural gas now have a smell added to it?
4. Find out what you should do if you smell natural gas.

These buildings were destroyed by a gas explosion in Germany.

5Ce States matter

What are the differences between the states of matter?

Everything around us is in one of the three states of matter. Each different state has a different set of properties.

1 What are the three states of matter?
2 Look at the photograph on the right. Name two solids.

This is a glacier, made of ice.

Squashing

Gases can be squashed easily. The air in the diver's tank has been squashed so that there is enough air in the tank for the diver to breathe for an hour underwater. The squashed gas takes up less room (has a smaller **volume**).

Liquids and solids cannot be squashed. The mechanical arm in the digger is filled with a liquid. When one end is pushed in the other end is pushed out.

3 Which of these things can be squashed into a smaller space?

carbon dioxide		water
wood	air	cooking oil

Flowing

Gases flow very easily and liquids also flow. When a volcano erupts, liquid lava pours down the mountain and the gases made by the volcano spread out into the air. The solid part of the volcano does not flow.

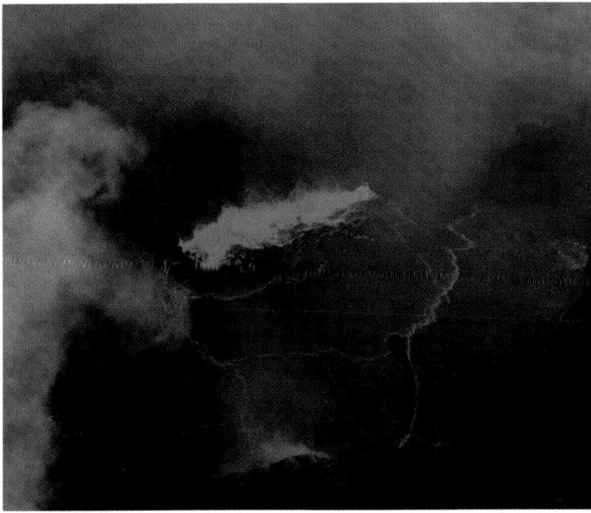

A volcano erupting.

4 A jar containing a brown gas and a blue liquid is dropped on the floor and breaks. Describe how the gas and the liquid would flow.

Changing shape

Liquids and gases change shape easily but solids do not. When the pipe in the photograph is finished it will carry **natural gas**, which will be able to flow around all the corners in the pipe because it can change shape. We burn natural gas in our homes for cooking and heating.

A natural gas pipeline being checked for leaks before it is buried underground.

5 Look at the photograph of the natural gas pipe.
  - a Why is it important that the pipe is checked for leaks?
  - b Can liquids be carried in pipes like the one in the photograph? Explain your answer.
  - c Can solids be carried in pipes like this? Explain your answer.

6 Lemonade is poured from a bottle into a glass. Describe how the shape of the lemonade changes.

7 Make a copy of this table and fill it in using ticks and crosses.

	Solids	Liquids	Gases
Can be squashed (can change volume)			
Flow easily			
Take up the shape of their containers			

You should know...

- Solids can't be squashed, have fixed shapes and do not flow.
- Liquids can't be squashed, but do not have fixed shapes and so can flow.
- Gases can be squashed. They do not have fixed shapes and flow very easily.

5Da Evaporation

How do liquids change into gases?

You can see puddles of water on the ground after it has been raining. After a while the puddles dry up because the water in the puddles has **evaporated**. This process is called **evaporation**.

Evaporation will soon make these puddles disappear.

When you wash clothes there is a lot of **liquid** water in them. When you hang the clothes up to dry, the water evaporates. It turns into a **gas** and then mixes with the gases in the air. You cannot see the water any more, but it is still there. When water is a gas it is called **water vapour**.

1 a What happens to the water in puddles when the puddles dry up?
  b What is this process called?

Liquids like perfume or aftershave evaporate easily. They turn into gases and mix with the air. You can smell aftershave when the gas reaches your nose.

2 Why can you smell perfume when you are near someone wearing it?
3 Why do you think you can smell coffee?

! Evaporation happens all around us. Over 1000 litres of water can evaporate from a tree in just one day!

You should know...

- Liquids change into gases by evaporation.
- Evaporated liquids mix with gases in the air.

5Da Focus on: Using evaporation

What happens when paint dries?

Paint is a mixture of water and a coloured substance, called **pigment**. Sometimes you add the water yourself with a brush, or mix a coloured powder with water. Some paints come ready-mixed. The paint is wet when you put it on the paper, then it dries as the water evaporates.

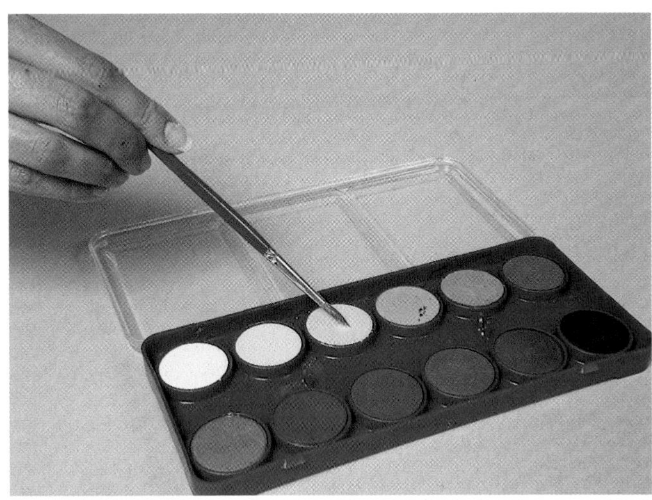

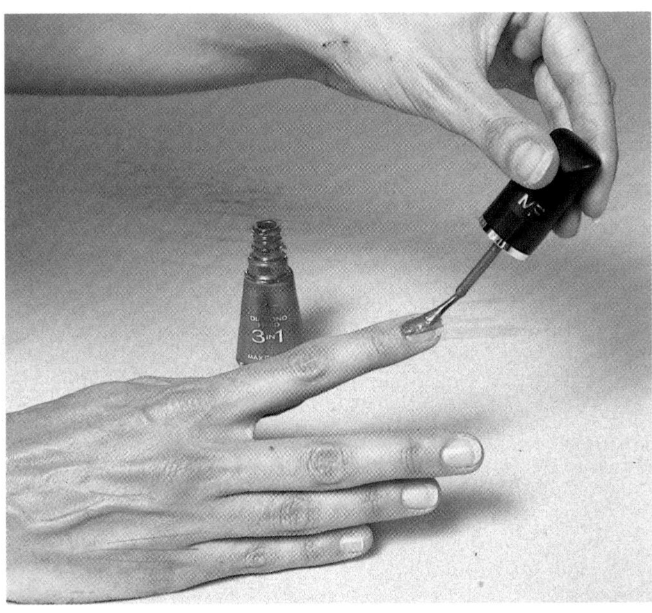

The pigment in paint mixes with the water. Some pigments do not mix with water very well and we have to use different liquids. Nail varnish, gloss paint and correction fluid all have different liquids mixed with the pigments. When the liquids evaporate they mix with the air. You can tell they are evaporating because many of these liquids are smelly!

Some liquids used in paint are bad for you if you breathe in too much of them. You need to open the windows if you are using gloss paint. This lets the evaporated liquid (**vapour**) escape from the room.

?

1 Why does paint need to be a liquid?
2 Paint is a mixture of which two things?
3 What happens when paint dries?
4 Why isn't water used in gloss paints?
5 Why should you open windows when you are using gloss paint?

5Db Investigating evaporation

How can we find out what affects evaporation?

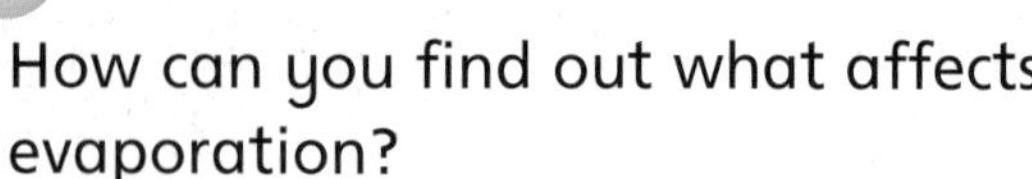

How can you find out what affects evaporation?

- What factors might make a difference?
- Which one will you investigate?
- How will you make your investigation fair?
- What equipment will you need?
- How will you record what happens?

Will a sunny day make the washing dry faster?

Would they dry better on a windy day?

5Db Dry it faster!

How can we make water evaporate quickly?

We often need to dry things like wet hair and wet clothes. If we want to dry them quickly, we need to make the water in them evaporate quickly.

When you peg out the washing on a washing line, you don't fold the washing up. This is because if all the wet clothes are flat there is a bigger area for the water to evaporate from. Water will evaporate faster when the area is bigger.

The clothes dry quickly on a warm, windy day. Water evaporates faster when it is warm. The wind also blows away the evaporated water so that more water can evaporate into the air.

You can use a tumble dryer to dry clothes quickly if it is cold or wet outside. A tumble dryer blows warm air through the clothes.

1 List three things that make water evaporate quickly.

2 A tumble dryer helps water to evaporate quickly in two ways. Explain how a tumble dryer helps to dry clothes.

3 Write an advert for a hairdryer. Your advert should explain what a hairdryer does and why this helps to dry hair quickly.

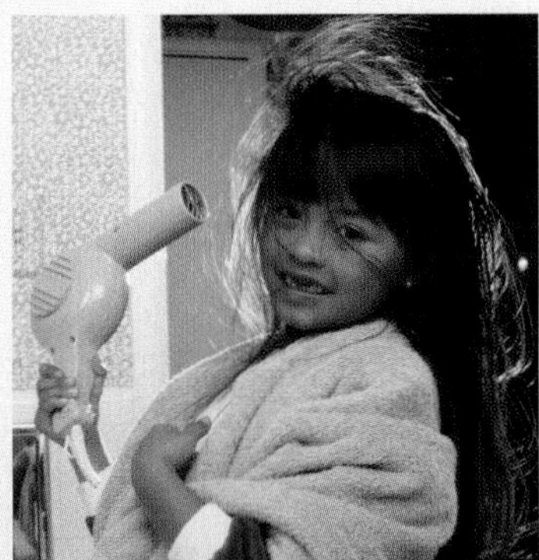

4 a What happens to the water on dishes when you dry them using a tea towel?

b What happens to the tea towel afterwards?

You should know...

- Evaporation happens faster if the water is warm, if there is a large area, and if the water vapour is blown away.

5Dc Condensation

How can a gas turn into a liquid?

The water in this kettle is being heated so it is evaporating quickly and changing to water vapour. The water vapour mixes with the air in the kettle, and then escapes from the kettle. You cannot see the water vapour, because it is a gas.

The air around the kettle is colder, so the water vapour cools down and turns back into liquid water. The cloud of 'steam' that you see is really lots of tiny drops of liquid water. The water has **condensed**.

You can often see water condensing in the bathroom. When you have a bath or shower, some of the hot water evaporates. When the water vapour touches a colder surface, like a mirror, it condenses. The tiny drops on the mirror are sometimes called **condensation**.

?

1 What happens to water vapour if it cools down?

2 The photograph shows two bath taps. Why can you only see condensation on one tap?

3 a Why do you often see condensation on kitchen windows in the winter?

b Why don't you see it very often in the summer?

How could you find out if Sally's idea is right?

An aeroplane's engines produce a lot of water vapour. The water vapour condenses when it gets into the cold air outside the aeroplane. It forms long trails which are made of tiny drops of liquid water.

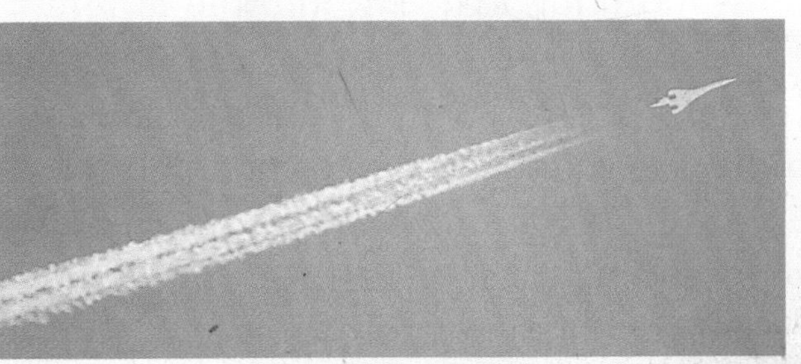

There is always some water vapour in the air around us. If you take a can of drink out of a fridge, you can usually see some drops of water on the outside of the can. The air near the can cools down, then the water vapour in the air condenses to form drops of liquid water.

Clouds can form when water vapour in the air cools down and condenses. Your breath can sometimes make clouds on a cold day. The heat from your body warms the air inside your lungs. Water evaporates from your lungs, and it stays as a gas while it is inside you. When you breathe the air out it cools down, and the water vapour condenses.

4 Explain why you often find drops of water on the outside of a can of cold drink.

5 a Why doesn't water vapour condense inside your lungs?

b Why can't you see your breath on a warm day?

6 a The trails behind aeroplanes are sometimes called 'contrails'. Why do you think they are called this?

b Some people call them 'vapour trails'. Why is this name not correct?

You should know...

- Gases change to liquids by condensation.
- Water vapour condenses when it cools down.

5Dd Changing state

What happens to the temperature when materials change state?

Most materials can exist in three different **states**. For example, water can exist as a solid (ice), a liquid (water), or a gas (water vapour). You can make materials change state by changing the temperature. For instance, if you heat ice it will **melt** when it reaches 0 °C. It changes state from a solid to a liquid. If you cool liquid water down to 0 °C it will **freeze** again. Changes of state can be reversed.

1 a What is the word that describes a gas changing into a liquid?
  b What does 'evaporating' mean?

2 a What is the melting point of ice?
  b What is the freezing point of water?

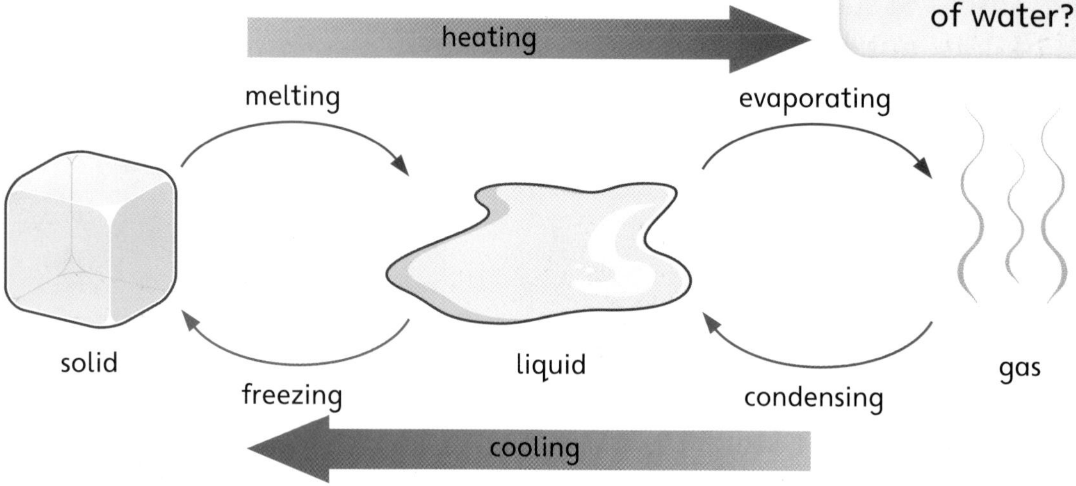

You can record the temperature of ice while it is melting. The graph shows the results you might get.

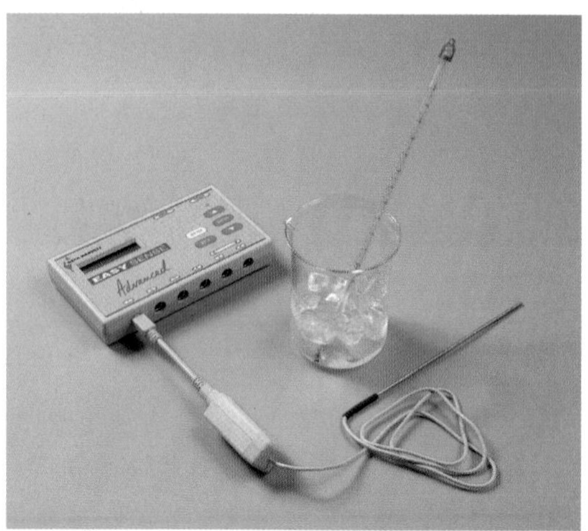

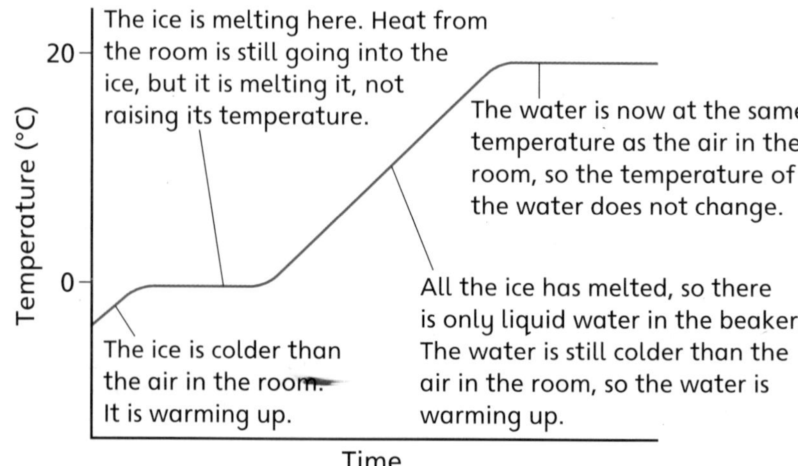

3 Look at the graph showing the temperature of melting ice. What temperature was the air in the room?

4 How could you make the water change back into ice?

Look at the graph on the opposite page. Predict what the graph would look like if you left the ice to melt in a much warmer room.

Liquid water can evaporate to form a gas. This can happen whenever the water is a liquid. Evaporation happens faster when the water is warmer. If water is heated to its boiling point of 100 °C, evaporation happens so fast that bubbles of gas form *inside* the liquid. You can see the liquid **boiling**.

The graph shows what happens to the temperature of water when it is heated to its boiling point.

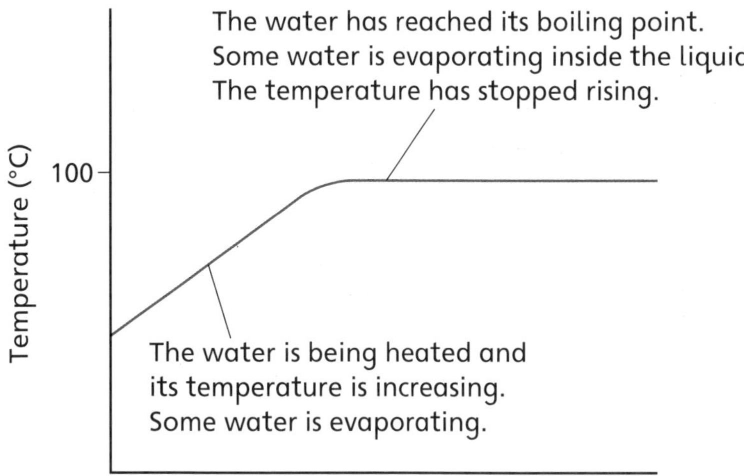

Bubbles of water vapour form in the water when it is boiling.

This does not happen! The temperature of liquid water never goes above 100 °C.

5 What is the boiling point of water?

6 Describe one difference between evaporation and boiling.

You should know...

- Changes of state can be reversed.
- Water melts at 0 °C and boils at 100 °C.
- Room temperature is about 20 °C.
- The temperature of water does not change while it is melting or boiling.

5De The water cycle

Where does our water come from?

You turn on a tap when you want water, but do you know how the water gets into the taps?

Water goes round in a cycle, from sea to clouds, then to rivers and back to the sea again. This is known as the **water cycle**.

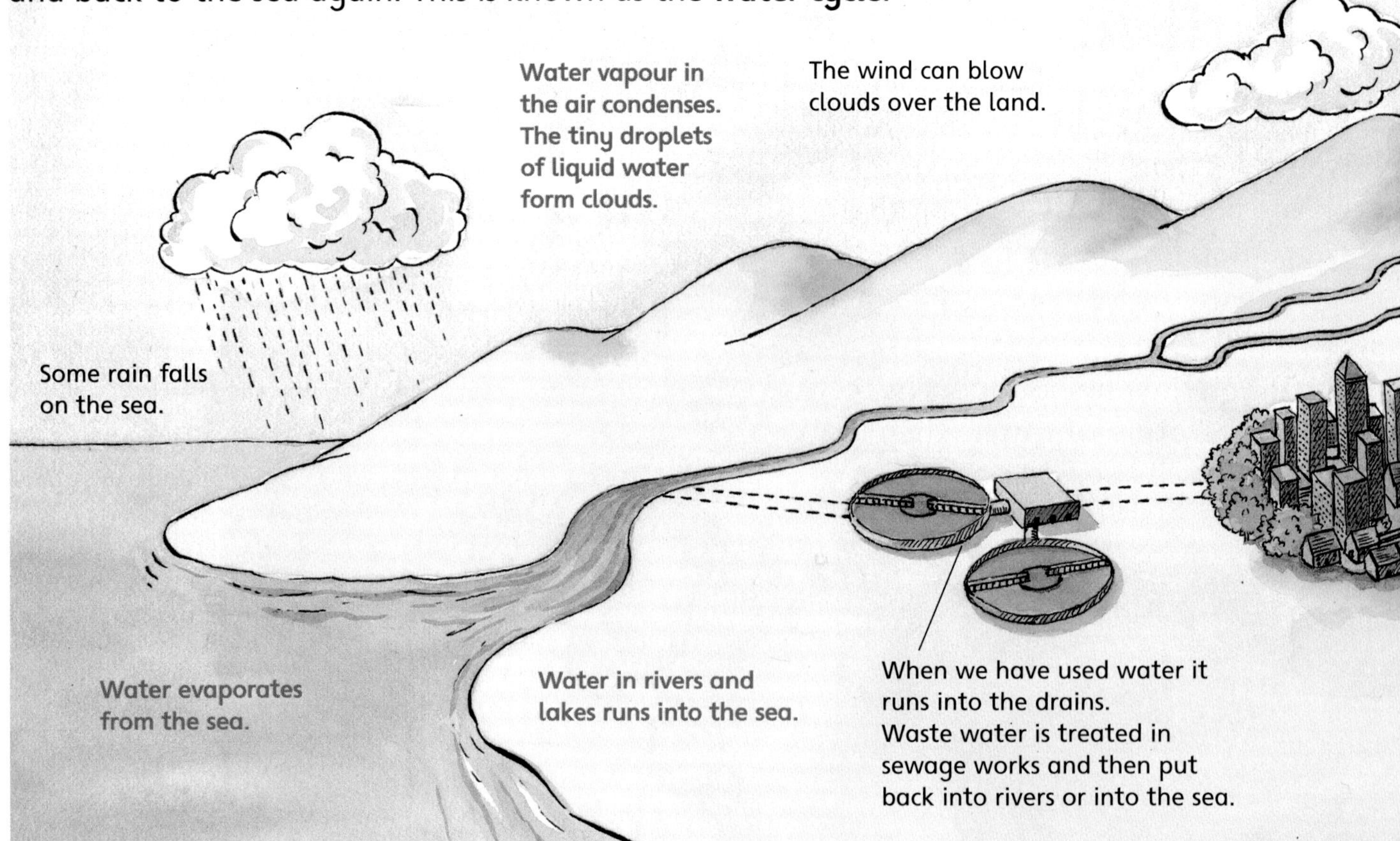

1 How does water from the sea get into the air?
2 How do clouds form?
3 What happens to water that falls on the land?
4 Where does the water in our taps come from?
5 Why are these changes called the 'water cycle'?
6 What kind of weather conditions will cause the most water to evaporate from the sea?
7 Describe the water cycle by recounting what happens to a drop of water from when it leaves the sea to when it returns to the sea.

If the air is cold, the water in clouds can fall as snow or hail.

Plants absorb water from the soil, and some of this evaporates.

The water in clouds can fall as rain.

Some water evaporates from lakes and rivers.

Sometimes people build dams to trap water in reservoirs.

Water runs into rivers and lakes.

Water is filtered and cleaned before it is sent to houses.

People can collect water from rivers or lakes.

Some water soaks into the ground. In some places, people dig wells to get the water.

People used to get their drinking water straight out of rivers, and their sewage went straight into the rivers. This caused a lot of diseases. The first time that drinking water was filtered in the UK was in 1825, when James Simpson of the Chelsea Water Company in London started to filter water through beds of sand.

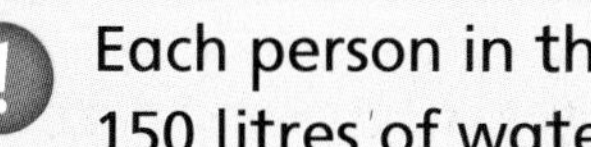

Each person in the UK uses about 150 litres of water every day!

You should know...

- What the water cycle is.
- How the water cycle depends on evaporation and condensation.

5De Focus on: Climate

Why is the weather different in different places?

Weather can be hot or cold, and it can be wet or dry. The **climate** of a place is its usual pattern of weather conditions. For instance, the climate in the United Kingdom is wet and **mild** (it never gets very hot or very cold).

If a place is near the Equator it will have a hot climate. If it is a long way north or south it will have a cold climate. However, the climate also depends on:

- how close the place is to the sea
- which way the winds blow
- whether there are any mountains nearby.

Air cools as it rises and the water vapour in it condenses. Most of the water falls as rain.

Air warms up again as it moves down.

warm, moist air

Air is pushed up over mountains.

sea

X

Y

?

1 Why is the air over the sea moist?
2 What happens to the temperature of the air as it flows up over the mountains?
3 Why do clouds form as the air rises?
4 a What would the climate be like at place X?
  b What would the climate be like at place Y? Explain your answer.

The highest mountains in the world are the Himalayas, between India and Tibet. These mountains have a big effect on the climate of India and Tibet.

UK

Africa

Equator

Indian Ocean

Australia

winds from the north east

TIBET

land above 3000 m

PAKISTAN

land below 1000 m

NEPAL

N W E S

INDIA

south westerly winds

BANGLADESH

The Himalayas.

Tibet is a very cold, dry country. Only about 430 mm of rain falls each year. The weather is similar all year round.

The climate in Tibet is cold and dry so there are not many plants for animals to eat.

The weather in India is much warmer and wetter. From June to September the winds blow from the south west. Up to 2400 mm of rain can fall on some places in northern India in these four months. In contrast, the UK gets an average of 1000 mm in a whole year. During the rest of the year the winds blow mainly from the north east, so not much rain falls on India.

India is very dry at some times of the year.

Sometimes there is too much rain in India, so floods destroy homes and damage farm land.

5 **a** Why does India have a lot of rain between June and September?
b What problems can this rain cause?
c Why is India much drier during the rest of the year?

6 Why doesn't Tibet have much rain at any time of the year?

7 What do you think the climate in Tibet would be like if the Himalayas did not exist?

5Ea The shape of the Earth

How do we know the shape of the Earth?

We live on the **Earth**. This photograph of the Earth was taken by astronauts on the Moon. It is easy to see from this photograph that the Earth is shaped like a **sphere**.

The first person to look at the Earth from space was Yuri Gagarin (1934–1968), in 1961.

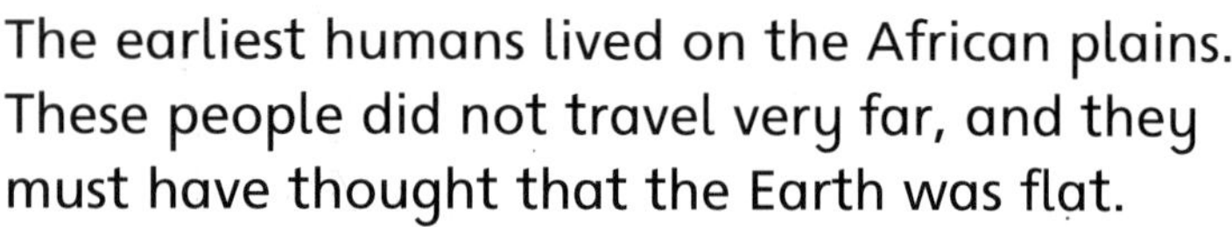

The earliest humans lived on the African plains. These people did not travel very far, and they must have thought that the Earth was flat.

People have known that the Earth is a sphere for over two thousand years, even though they could not go into space to look at it from a distance. They used other **observations** as **evidence** for their ideas.

Humans travelled long distances to trade, and even built ships to let them sail to lands beyond the sea. People noticed that the bottom part of a ship disappeared first when the ship sailed away, and the tops of the sails disappeared last of all. This would not happen if the Earth were flat.

?

1 Which of these things is a sphere?
   A a plate
   B a football
   C a box

2 a How did sailing ships help people to know that the Earth is a sphere?
   b Why couldn't these people just look at a photograph of the Earth?

Scientists also noticed that shadows are different in different places.

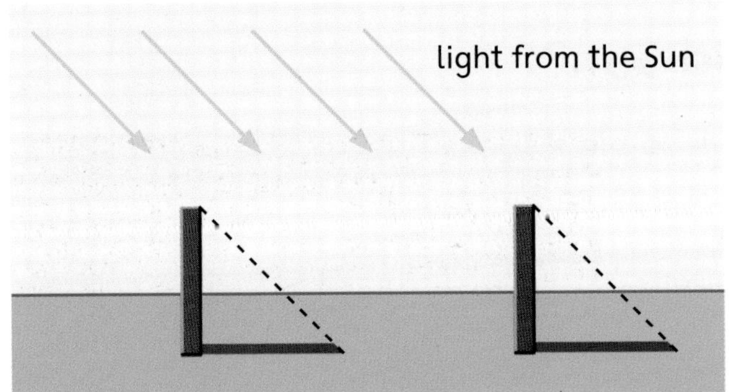

If the Earth were flat, a stick would have the same length shadow everywhere.

The different shadows can be explained if the Earth is a sphere.

3 How can shadows in different places show that the Earth is not flat?

The first ship to sail all the way round the world was the *Victoria*. It set off from Portugal in 1519, with four other ships. Only the *Victoria* survived, and returned to Portugal three years later. At that time most educated people knew that the Earth was a sphere, but many ordinary people did not. Some of the sailors were afraid that they would fall off the edge of the world. When they arrived back in Portugal, more people were convinced that the Earth was a sphere.

The Victoria.

4 Write down one reason why we know that the Moon is spherical.

The Moon and the Sun are also spherical. From the Earth, we can only see that they are round – we cannot tell if they are spheres, or flat discs like CDs. Photographs taken from space make it easier to see that the Moon and Sun are spherical.

You should know...

- The Earth, Moon and Sun are all spherical.
- Some of the reasons why we know the Earth is a sphere.

Astronauts have flown right around the Moon.

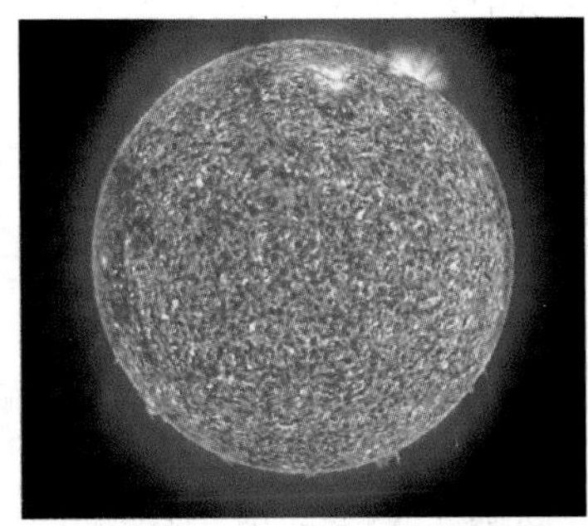
The Sun is spherical.

5Eb The size of the Earth

How big are the Earth, Moon and Sun?

The Earth is very big. It is a sphere, but because it is so big it looks flat to us when we stand on it. You cannot see that it is a sphere unless you are a long way from it.

*You cannot tell from here that the Earth is curved. The **horizon** looks straight.*

Some aeroplanes fly so high that the people inside can see that the horizon is curved.

1 Why does the Earth look flat to us?

The diameter of the Earth is nearly 13 000 kilometres. The Moon is smaller than the Earth – its diameter is nearly 4000 kilometres.

The Moon is a long way from the Earth, but it is much closer to the Earth than the Sun.

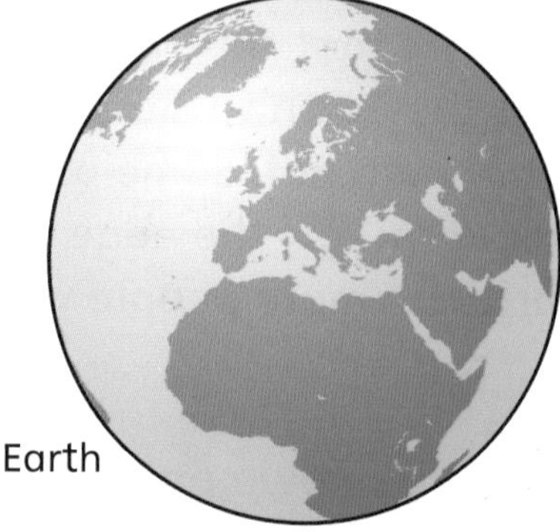

Earth Moon

Sun – 1000 'Earths' away

You could fit 30 'Earths' between the Earth and the Moon.

If you drew the Sun to the same scale, you could fit over 1000 'Earths' in between the Sun and the Earth!

The Sun is much bigger than the Earth and the Moon. The diameter of the Sun is 1 400 000 km. It is over a hundred times bigger than the Earth, and 400 times bigger than the Moon. The Moon and the Sun look about the same size from the Earth, but that is only because the Sun is much further away from the Earth than the Moon.

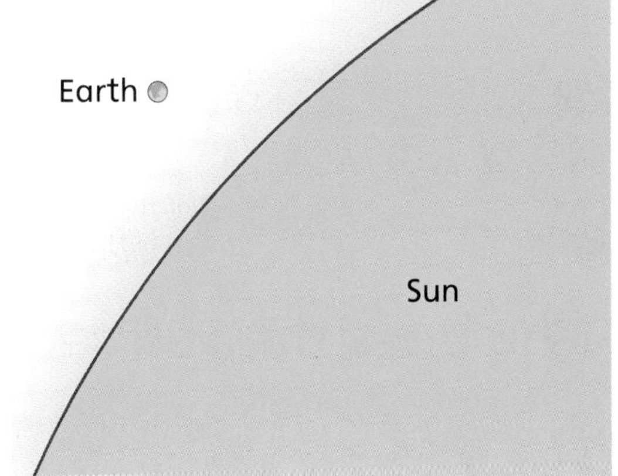

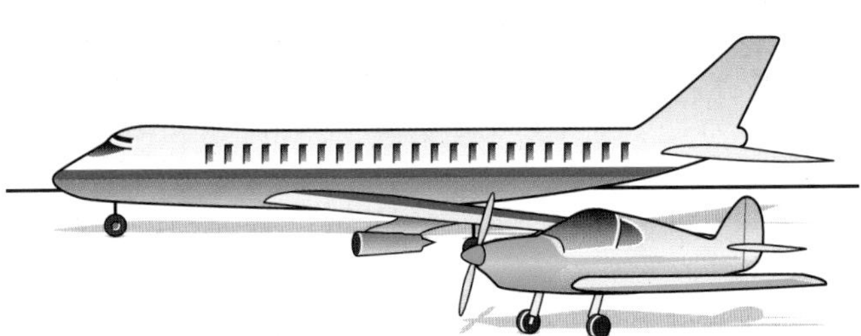

The airliner is much bigger than the small aeroplane.

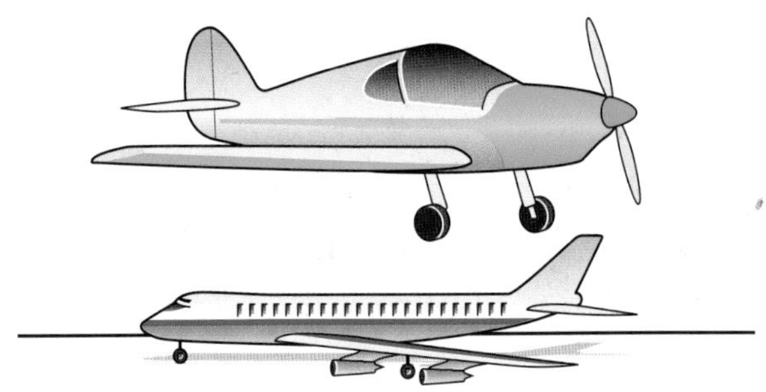

In this picture the airliner looks small, because it is a long way off.

The Sun is very hot.
The temperature on its surface is 6000 °C. We can feel the heat from the Sun here on Earth, nearly 150 million kilometres away!

2 Write these things in order of size, starting with the biggest.

Earth	Sun	Moon

3 Which is the closest to the Earth; the Sun or the Moon?

4 Why does the Sun seem to be about the same size as the Moon?

How could you make a scale model to show the Earth, the Sun and the Moon?

- What information would you need?
- What materials would you need?

You should know...

- How big the Moon and the Sun are, compared to the Earth.
- How far away the Sun is from the Earth, compared to the Moon.

5Ec What is moving?

Why does the Sun seem to move across the sky?

If you could watch the Sun all day, you would see that it seems to move across the sky.

The Sun rises in the east in the morning.

The Sun is in the south in the middle of the day.

The Sun sets in the west in the evening.

How can you find out how the Sun seems to move without looking at it?

NEVER look directly at the Sun. It can damage your eyes.

The moving shadow is **evidence** that the Sun seems to move across the sky. There are two different ways of explaining this evidence.

?

1. Why should you never look directly at the Sun?
2. How can you use shadows to find out how the Sun seems to move?

The Sun could be moving around the Earth.

not to scale

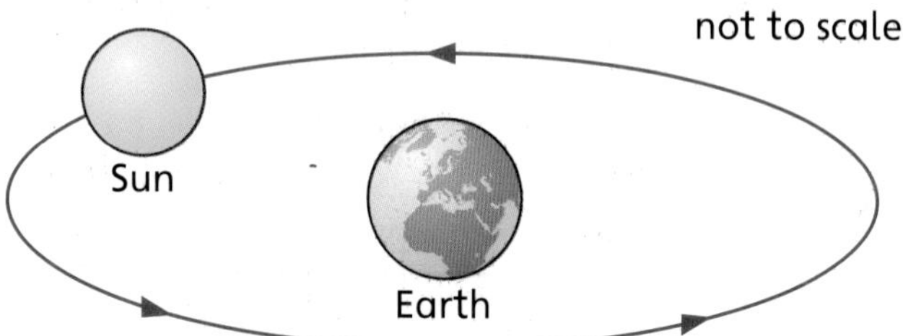

The Earth could be spinning.

not to scale

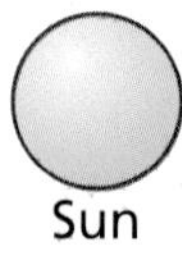

You cannot tell which of these explanations is correct just by watching the Sun. However, scientists have made other observations of stars and planets in the sky. The idea that the Earth is spinning helps to explain all these other observations as well.

The Sun *seems* to move, because we are living on a planet that is moving. This is a bit like going on a car journey – the houses that you are going past look as though they are moving, but it is really the car that is moving. We still talk about the Sun 'rising' and 'setting', even though it is the Earth that is moving.

3 a Write down two different explanations for why the Sun seems to move across the sky.
  b Which explanation is the correct one?
4 Why isn't it really correct to say that the Sun 'rises'?

You are moving at about 1000 km/h just by sitting still, because the Earth you are sitting on is spinning.

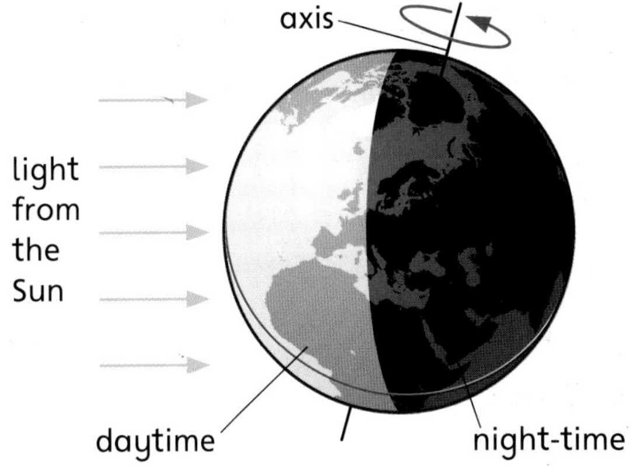

It takes 24 hours for the Earth to spin once on its **axis**. The axis is an imaginary line through the centre of the Earth. It is daytime in the part of the Earth facing the Sun, and it is night-time in the part of the Earth facing away from the Sun.

The Sun rises at different times in the summer and in the winter.

Summer.

Winter.

5 How long does it take the Earth to spin once?
6 Why do we have day and night?
7 a Does the Sun rise early or late on a winter morning?
  b Does the Sun set early or late on a summer evening?

You should know...

- The Sun rises in the east and sets in the west.
- The Sun seems to move because the Earth is spinning.
- Why we have day and night.

5Ec Investigating sunrise and sunset

Is there a pattern in sunrise and sunset through the year?

How can you find out if there is a pattern in the times of sunrise and sunset during the year?

- Which factors could change during the year?
- Which factor will you investigate?
- What patterns do you think there might be?
- How will you collect your information?
- How will you present your information to see if there is a pattern?

We get more hours of daylight in the summer than we do in winter.

The Sun never rises before 6 o'clock in the morning.

The Sun sets in different places at different times of the year.

Evenings are lighter in the summer.

I think the Sun always rises in the east.

5Ec Focus on: Sundials

How can you tell the time without a clock?

Mechanical clocks were not invented until the 1300s. For thousands of years before then, people had been telling the time using candle clocks, water clocks, or **sundials**.

Sundials have a central stick, called a **gnomon** (pronounced '***no***-*mon*'), and a **dial** with hours marked on it. As the Earth spins, the shadow of the gnomon moves around the dial and shows the time. The sundial has to be lined up properly, so that it reads the correct time.

The height of the Sun in the sky changes with the seasons, so the gnomon has to be tilted to make sure that the sundial always shows the correct time.

There are lots of different kinds of sundial. Sometimes sundials are put on walls. There were even portable sundials, which were the equivalent of today's wristwatches!

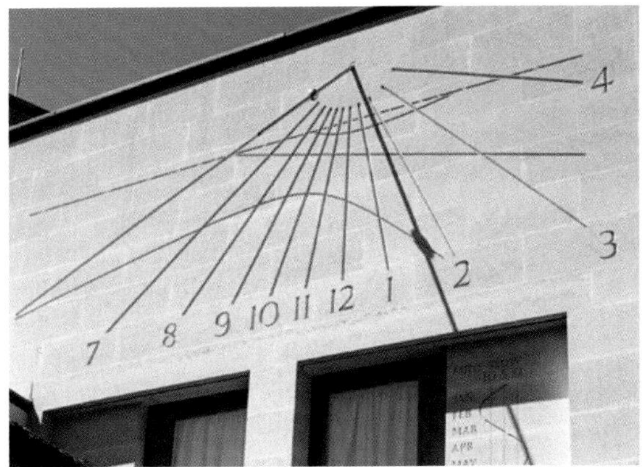

This is a modern sundial.

This is a portable sundial. It has a compass built into it.

1 What is a gnomon?
2 Why is the gnomon on a sundial tilted?
3 Why do you think the modern sundial was built?
4 Why does the portable sundial need a compass?
5 There are disadvantages to using a sundial to tell the time. Write down as many disadvantages as you can.
6 Find out about other ways of telling the time, such as water clocks and candle clocks.

5Ed Years

What is a year?

You measure how old you are in years. A **year** is the time from one birthday to the next one, or the time from one Christmas to the next. If you counted each day between your birthdays, you would find that a year is 365 days long.

People first measured years because it was important to plant their crops in the right season. The pattern in sunrise and sunset times also changes over a year.

The Sun is higher in the sky in the summer than in the winter. If you measure the shadow of something at 12 o'clock every day, it is shortest in the middle of summer. It takes 365 days for the shadow to become its shortest again.

The Sun is high in the sky in the summer, so the shadow of the stick is short. It is low in the sky in winter, so the shadow is longer.

1 How many days are there in a year?
2 How do sunset times change between summer and winter?

The changes in the seasons and in the height of the Sun happen because the Earth is moving around the Sun. The path of the Earth around the Sun is called an **orbit**. It takes $365\frac{1}{4}$ days, or one year, for the Earth to orbit the Sun once. We account for the $\frac{1}{4}$ days by having an extra day once every four years. The years with an extra day in them are called **leap years**.

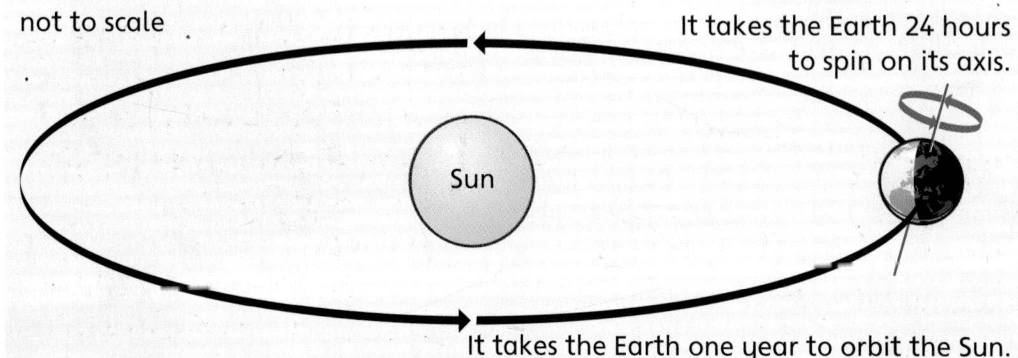

3 a How does the length of a shadow change during the year?
  b Why does this happen?
4 How long does it take for the Earth to go around the Sun once?

You should know...

- The Earth moves around the Sun.
- It takes the Earth one year to orbit the Sun.

5Ed Focus on: Seasons

Why do we have summer and winter?

There are lots of differences between summer and winter.

1 Describe how the weather is different in the summer and the winter.
2 What differences can you see in plants in the two seasons?
3 a How does the length of daylight change from summer to winter?
  b How does the height of the Sun in the sky change with the seasons?
(*Hint:* You might need to look back at pages 58–59 and 62.)

These changes happen because the Earth's axis is tilted. When it is summer in the UK, the **North Pole** is tilted towards the Sun. The North Pole is tilted away from the Sun when it is winter in the UK.

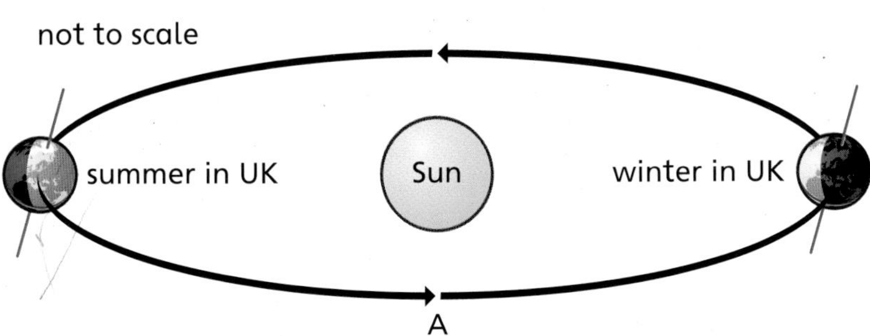

4 Look at the diagram of the Earth's orbit. When the Earth is at point A:
  a what season will it be
  b how long will the daylight last compared to the summer
  c how high in the sky will the Sun be, compared to the winter?
5 Find out what season it is in Australia when it is summer in the UK. Try to explain your answer.
6 Find out what the 'midnight sun' is, and where and when you can see it.

When the North Pole is tilted towards the Sun, the Sun is high in the sky in the middle of the day and the days are longer than the nights.

In summer, the angle between the Sun and the horizon is large.

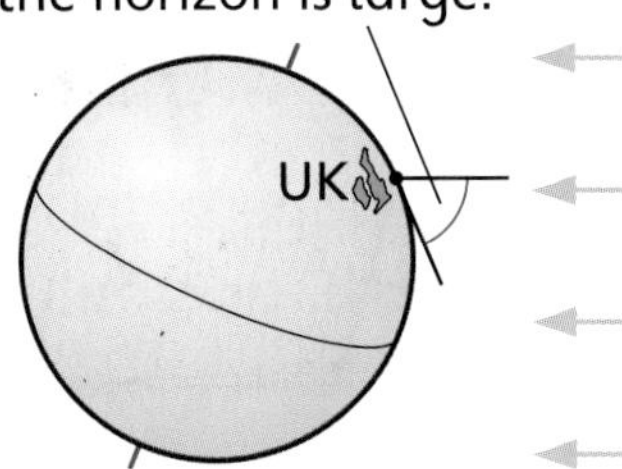

In winter, the angle between the Sun and the horizon is quite small.

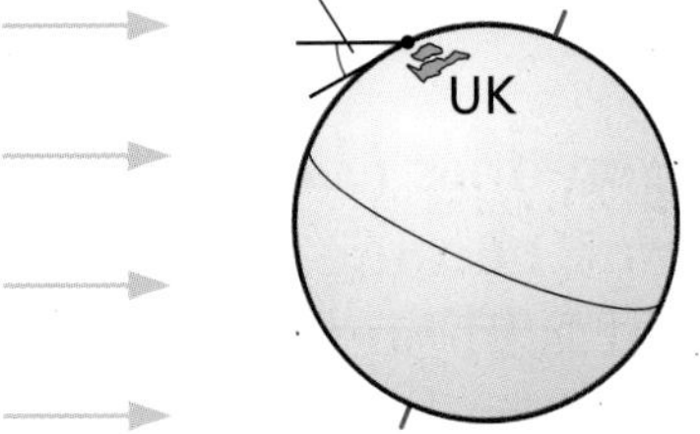

5Ee The Moon

How does the Moon move?

The Moon does not always seem to be the same shape. It can look like a complete circle, a thin crescent, or something in between. These shapes are called **phases of the Moon**.

*When the Moon looks like a complete circle we call it a **full moon**.*

*When the Moon is just a thin crescent we call it a **new moon**.*

Sometimes the Moon is not quite a full circle.

The appearance of the Moon changes in a regular pattern. It takes 28 days for the pattern to repeat itself. This is because it takes approximately 28 days for the Moon to **orbit** (go around) the Earth.

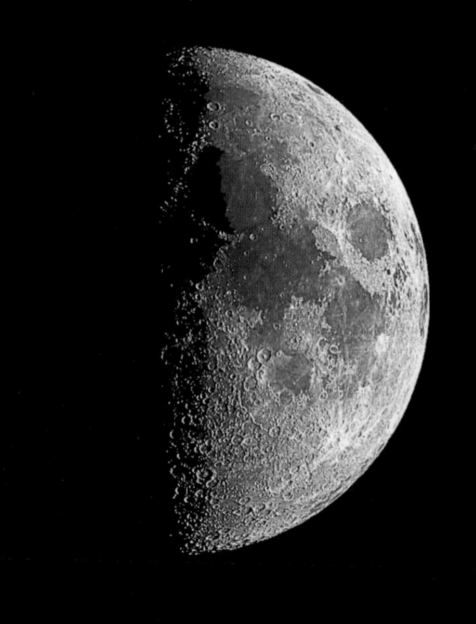

?

1 Look carefully at the photographs of the Moon, then choose the correct answer.
You can see the Moon...
A only in the daytime.
B in the day or at night.
C only at night.

2 How many days are there between one full Moon and the next?

The Moon does not really change shape. The shape seems to change because it is moving around the Earth, and only half of it is lit by the Sun.

We always see the same side of the Moon, because it takes the same time to spin on its axis as it takes to orbit the Earth.

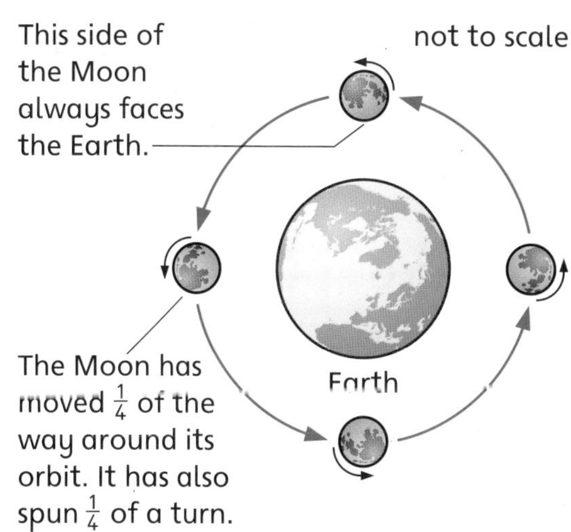

3 How long does it take for the Moon to spin on its axis once?

4 Why does the Moon seem to be different shapes?

How does this model help you to understand the phases of the Moon?

No-one knew what the back of the Moon looked like until 1959, when an unmanned spacecraft called Lunik 3 flew behind the Moon and sent pictures back to Earth.

The Moon is very different to the Earth. There is no air and no water, so there are no plants and animals. The surface of the Moon is covered in rocks and dust.

Only 12 people have ever been to the Moon. The astronauts had to wear space suits.

5 Why did astronauts need to wear space suits when they visited the Moon?

6 Find out about the astronauts who visited the Moon, and how they got there and back. You could start by looking up the word 'Apollo'.

You should know...

- The Moon takes 28 days to orbit the Earth.
- The appearance of the Moon seems to change because it is orbiting the Earth.

5Fa Making sounds

How are sounds made?

Sounds are all around us. Lorries, cars and aeroplanes make sounds. We can make sounds with our bodies, by talking, singing or clapping.

Musical instruments can make many different sounds.

P

How can you use these objects to make sounds?

- What happens to each object when it is making a sound?

?

1 a Write down five different things that can make sounds.
  b Describe how each thing makes sounds.

Sounds are made when something **vibrates** (moves backwards and forwards quickly). If you make a sound using an elastic band or a ruler, you can see the vibrations. You cannot see the vibrations you make when you talk, but you can feel them.

You can feel vibrations if you put your fingers on your throat when you talk.

*This is the inside of a **loudspeaker**. It converts electricity into sounds. You cannot see the vibrations it makes. If you put sand on the loudspeaker, the vibrations make the sand jump about.*

?

2 What are vibrations?
3 What vibrates when a guitar is played?
4 A loudspeaker vibrates when it makes a sound. How can you show this?
5 There are lots of words that we can use to describe sounds.
  a Make a list of sound words like scream, bang, crash.
  b Write a short story or poem that uses some of these words.

You should know...

- Sounds are made when objects vibrate.

5Fa Focus on: Animal sounds

How do animals make sounds?

Humans have a **larynx** (pronounced '*lar-inks*') in the tube that takes air to and from the lungs. The larynx is the bit that bobs up and down when we swallow. Inside the larynx are bands called **vocal cords**. These vibrate when we speak or sing. Many other animals, like dogs and cows, make sounds in the same way.

A meadow grasshopper.

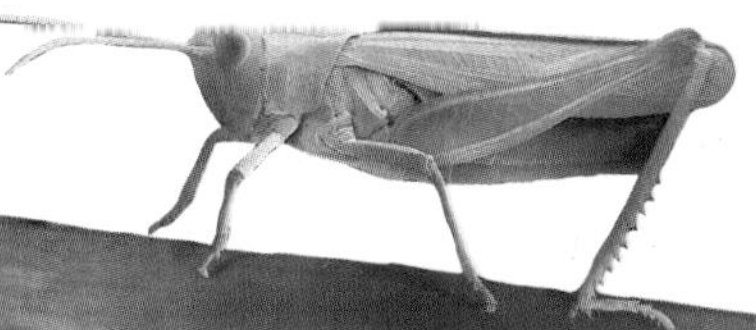

Grasshoppers do not use vocal cords to help them to make sound. Grasshoppers rub their back legs against their wings or body, and the vibrations caused by this rubbing make a sound. Males use the 'songs' to attract females and to warn other males to stay away.

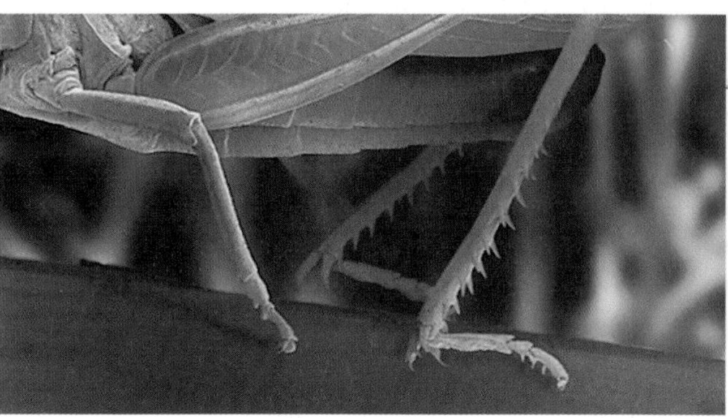

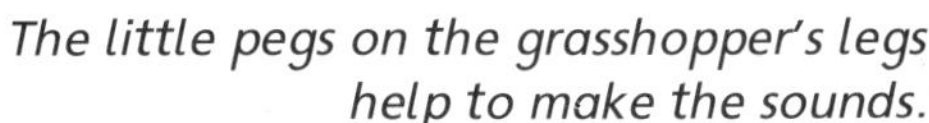

The little pegs on the grasshopper's legs help to make the sounds.

A whale can make sounds using its larynx, but it can also make a noise by leaping out of the water. The noise whales make when they crash back into the sea can be heard several kilometres away. Scientists are not sure why they do this – it may be to communicate with other whales, or it may help to stun nearby fish so that the whale can catch them.

All the sounds mentioned so far are sounds that the animals make on purpose, to communicate. Sometimes animals make noises because they are doing other things. This hummingbird has to flap its wings very fast to hover near the flower. Its wings make a humming noise.

A hummingbird hovering.

?

1 How do humans make sounds when they sing?
2 How do grasshoppers make sounds?
3 How can a whale make a noise without using its larynx?
4 Why do hummingbirds hum?

5Fb Moving sounds

Which materials can sound travel through?

You hear sounds when their **vibrations** travel to your ears. Most of the sounds you hear have travelled through the air. Air is a **gas**. Sound can travel through all gases.

When you talk to your friends, the sounds you make travel through the air.

Sound can travel through **solids**. You can hear noises outside your classroom, even if the door is shut. The sounds can travel through glass, bricks and wood.

When you use a 'string telephone' the sound travels through the string, which is a solid.

?

1 Write down the name of one gas that sound can travel through.
2 Write down the names of five different solid materials that sound can travel through.

! Evelyn Glennie is a musician. Evelyn is deaf, so she cannot hear what she is playing very well with her ears. She can play well because she can feel, with other parts of her body, the vibrations her instruments are making, and she can see the vibrations on some instruments.

Sound can also travel through **liquids**. If you swim underwater, or put your ears under the water when you are in the bath, you can still hear things. Vibrations travel through the water to your ears.

Whales make sounds underwater. Some whale 'songs' can be heard up to 160 km away.

How could you find out which materials sound travels through best?

- How can you measure the sound?
- How can you make your test fair?
- How will you present your results?

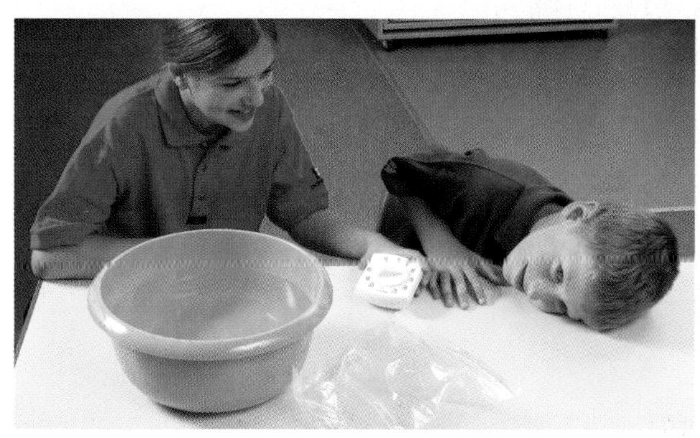

Francis Hauksbee (1666–1713) was the first person to show that sound needs a material to travel through.

Sound has to have a material to travel through. There is no air in space, so you would not be able to hear this astronaut if she were talking.

Sound takes time to travel. Sound takes one second to travel 330 metres in air.

3 Why can't you hear an astronaut talking in space?

4 This table shows how fast sound travels through different materials.

Material	Speed (m/s)
metal	6000
brick	3000
water	1500
air	330

a Which two materials in the table are solids?

b Which material is a gas?

c Plot a bar chart to show these speeds.

d Does sound travel fastest in solids, liquids or gases?

It takes one-third of a second for the sound of the starting gun to reach the end of a 100 m running track.

You should know...

- We hear things when vibrations travel to our ears.
- Sound needs a material to travel through.
- Sound vibrations can travel through solids, liquids and gases.

5Fc Controlling noise

How can we stop sound travelling?

Lots of things around us make sounds. We need to hear some sounds, like the sound of someone talking to us, and we like to listen to musical sounds. However, some sounds are annoying, and if sounds are very loud they can damage our ears.

Very loud music can damage our ears.

1 a Write down three different sounds that you like to hear.
  b Write down three different sounds that could damage your ears.

There are lots of things at home that make a noise. You don't want to hear the washing machine working in the kitchen, or hear music that someone is playing in another room. Soft materials, like carpets or curtains, can **absorb** some of the vibrations, and make the sound quieter.

Sometimes you cannot stop things making sounds. If you have to go close to noisy machinery you need to protect your ears. You can do this by wearing **ear plugs** or **ear defenders**.

The doors and roof of this car are lined with soft materials that help to absorb sounds made by the engine and by other cars.

2 a Write down two things in a house that can absorb vibrations.
  b How do car makers try to make cars quiet inside?

The machines in this factory make a lot of noise. The woman has to wear ear defenders so that her hearing is not damaged.

3 Why do workers in some factories have to wear ear protection?
4 Why shouldn't you spend too long dancing next to the loudspeakers at a disco?

How can scientists find out when people in noisy places need to wear ear plugs?

- What information would they need?
- How would they collect the information?

The vibrations spread out from a source of sound, so the sound is quieter if you are further away. An aeroplane's engines make a lot of noise, but when the aeroplane is high in the sky you can hardly hear it.

*People who work at airports have to wear **ear protection** because they have to go close to aeroplanes which have their engines running.*

5 Airport workers have to wear ear protection. Why do you think that the passengers inside the aeroplane do not need to wear ear protection?
6 People who talk on the telephone as part of their job often wear microphones like the one in the photograph.
   a When the man speaks, what do the vibrations have to travel through to get to the microphone?
   b Look at the picture of the man with the throat microphone. The throat microphone lets him talk to other people when it is very noisy. When he speaks, what do the vibrations travel through to get to the microphone?
   c Explain why a throat microphone is best when it is very noisy.

You should know...

- Loud noises can damage your ears.
- Soft materials can be used to absorb vibrations.
- People working in noisy places need to protect their ears.

5Fc Investigating soundproofing

Which materials are best at absorbing sound?

P

How can you find out which materials are best at absorbing sound?

- What will you use as your source of sound?
- Which materials will you test?
- How will you measure the sound?
- How will you make sure your test is fair?

5Fc Focus on: Ears

How do our ears work?

Our ears include bones and tubes inside our skulls as well as the parts we can see sticking out.

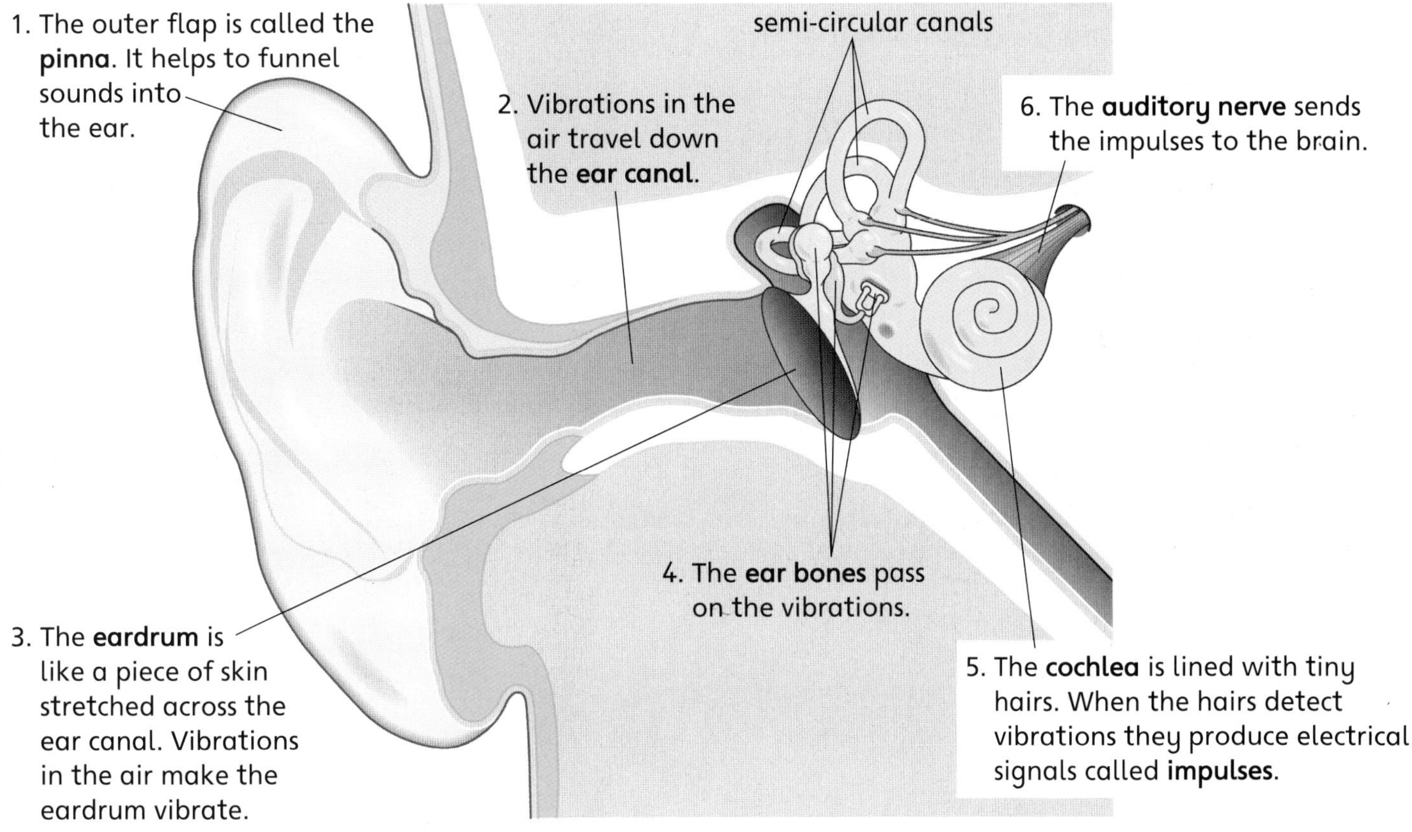

Sudden loud sounds can damage the eardrum. Constant loud noise, such as working in a very noisy place, or playing a personal stereo too loudly, can permanently damage the cochlea.

?

1 Draw a table like this, and fill it in to show all the parts of the ear and what each one does.

Name of part	What it does
pinna	funnels sounds into the ear canal

2 Write down two ways in which your ears can be damaged.

3 Find out what the semi-circular canals do.

5Fd Changing sounds

How can we make different sounds?

You can make lots of different sounds using musical instruments. A sound can be high or low, and it can be loud or quiet. The **pitch** of a sound describes whether it is a high or low sound.

You can make loud sounds on musical instruments by hitting them harder, or plucking strings harder.

You can make high or low sounds on a xylophone by hitting different bars. Each bar makes a sound with a different pitch. The short bars make high-pitched sounds.

1 a How can you make a quiet sound on a xylophone?

  b How can you make a low-pitched sound on a xylophone?

2 These are tubular bells. Which bell will make a sound with the highest pitch?

Drums make sounds when you hit the skin to make it vibrate. Small drums make high-pitched sounds, and large drums make low-pitched sounds.

C

How can you change the pitch of the sounds on these instruments?

- How can you change the loudness of the sounds?

Some drums have screws around the edge. The screws can be used to tighten the drum skin. When the skin is tighter, it makes a higher pitched sound.

A kettledrum.

3 Look at the picture of the kettledrum.
   a How could you make it give a loud sound?
   b How could you make it give a lower-pitched sound?

Guitars have strings that vibrate when you pluck them. Each string on a guitar makes a different pitched sound because it is a different thickness. Thick strings make lower sounds than thin strings.

The guitar has pegs at one end. The pegs can be used to adjust the tightness of the strings. If a string is tightened up, the sound it makes gets higher.

The person playing a guitar can change the length of a string by putting a finger on it so that only part of the string can vibrate. Shorter strings make higher-pitched sounds.

4 Which string will make the lowest sound:
   a a long one or a short one
   b a tight one or a loose one
   c a thin one or a thick one?

5 Look at the picture of the person playing the guitar. Write down two ways that he could play a higher sound without changing the tightness of the strings.

You should know...

- What pitch means.
- The pitch of a drum depends on how big it is and how tight its skin is.
- The pitch of a string depends on its thickness, length and how tight it is.

5Fe Air sounds

How can we use air to make different sounds?

Pan pipes are made of tubes of different lengths. You can make music with them by blowing across the tops of the tubes, which makes the air inside the tubes vibrate. Each tube makes a different sound. The short tubes make sounds with a high pitch.

Which bottle will make the highest pitched sound?

- Explain your prediction.

Trombone players make a buzzing sound with their lips. The sound travels through the air in the tubes and comes out sounding quite different. The player can make loud sounds by blowing harder. The pitch of the sound is changed by moving the slide in and out to change the length of the tube. The length of the vibrating air inside the trombone is called the **air column**.

?

1 Which tubes in a set of pan pipes make the lowest sounds?
2 What makes the vibrations when someone plays a trombone?
3 Does a trombone player have to make the tube longer or shorter to make a high-pitched sound?

Instruments that use vibrating air to make a sound are called **wind instruments**. Recorders are wind instruments. When you play a recorder you cover or uncover different holes to make different sounds. The lowest sounds are made when all the holes are covered up, because then the air column is longest.

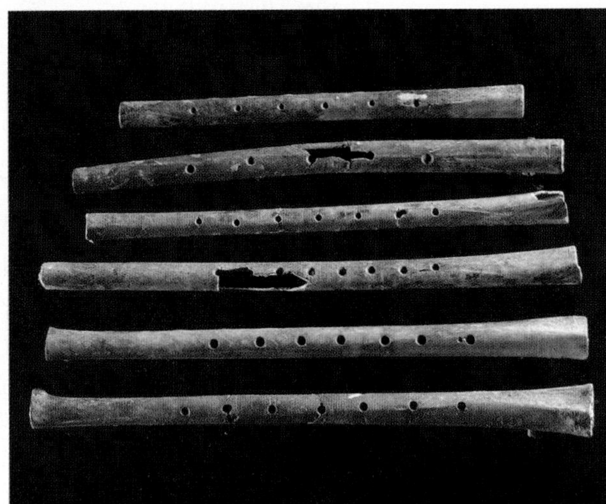

These are the oldest complete flutes that have been found. They are 9000 years old, and were found in China. However, some scientists think that some 80 000 year old bones with holes in them are part of a flute. People have been playing musical instruments for a long time!

Some wind instruments are more complicated than recorders. They have keys to help the players cover up different combinations of holes.

Wind instruments come in different sizes. A piccolo is much smaller than a flute.

4 Why do you get the lowest sound from a recorder when all the holes are covered up?

5 Do you think a flute or a piccolo can play the highest sound? Explain your answer.

6 Find out how the vibrations are made in clarinets and oboes.

You should know...

- Some instruments use vibrating air to make sounds.
- Different sounds can be made in wind instruments by changing the length of the air column.

Glossary

absorb	Take in, such as when something soft takes in sound and does not let it pass through.
addictive	Things that are addictive make you feel that you cannot cope without them.
air column (*kol-um*)	The length of air inside a wind instrument.
air resistance	When air slows down things that are moving through it.
alcohol (*alk-O-holl*)	The drug in drinks that are bought in pubs (e.g. beer and wine).
anther	Part of a flower that makes pollen grains.
argon	A gas that is in the air. It is used in light bulbs.
artery	A blood vessel carrying blood away from your heart.
auditory nerve	Carries signals (impulses) from the cochlea to the brain.
axis	The imaginary line that the Earth is spinning around.
balance	A piece of apparatus used to measure mass.
balanced diet	Eating a wide range of foods to give you all the food groups you need without having too much of any one food group.
biceps (*bye-seps*)	A muscle in your upper arm which contracts to lift your lower arm.
beats per minute	The units used to measure pulse rates.
blood vessel	A tube that carries blood in your body.
boiling	A liquid evaporating as fast as it can.
bones	Your skeleton is made out of hard pieces called bones.
breeding	Helping animals to reproduce.
calcium (*cal-see-um*)	A mineral that is needed to make bones and teeth.
carbohydrate (*car-bO-hy-drate*)	A food group that gives you energy. There are two types of carbohydrate, sugar and starch.
carbon dioxide	A gas found in the air. It is used in fizzy drinks.
carbon monoxide	A poisonous gas that you cannot smell or see. It can be produced by natural gas fires and boilers if they are not properly maintained.
carpel	The female organ of the flower. It is made up of the stigma, the style and the ovary.
climate	The usual pattern of weather conditions in a particular place.
cochlea (*cok-lee-a*)	Part of the ear that produces signals (impulses) when it detects sound.
condensation (*con-den-say-shun*)	The process where a gas condenses into a liquid, or the tiny drops of water produced when water vapour touches a cold surface such as a mirror.
condense	A gas turning into a liquid.
contract (*con-tract*)	Squash up or get shorter.
coronary artery	Blood vessel that supplies the heart muscle with blood.
dial	A scale on which the hours are marked on a sundial.
diet	The scientific word for what you eat.
drug	A substance that has an effect on the way your body works.
ear bones	Tiny bones in the ear which pass on vibrations from the eardrum to the cochlea.
ear canal	A tube in the ear which sounds travel down.
eardrum	A piece of skin stretched across the ear canal. It vibrates when vibrations (sounds) reach it.
ear defenders	Pads of material worn on the ears to stop sound getting in.
ear plugs	Small pieces of material (such as foam) put into the ear to stop sound getting in.
ear protection (*pro-tek-shun*)	Anything used to stop loud sounds damaging the ears.
Earth	The planet on which we live.
egg	Female part of a plant which joins with a pollen grain in fertilisation. Also called an ovum.
evaporate	A liquid turning into a gas.
evaporation (*ev-vap-or-ay-shun*)	The process where a liquid changes into a gas.
evidence	Information that helps us to know that something is true, or makes us believe a particular idea.
extinct	When a type of animal or plant no longer exists it is said to be extinct.
factor	Something that changes what happens in an experiment.
fair test	An experiment when only one factor is changed.

fat	A food group that gives you energy. Fats feel greasy.
fertilisation (*fert-ill-eyes-**ay**-shun*)	When the male pollen grain joins with the female ovum (or egg).
fibre (*__fy__-ber*)	Part of your food which passes through you. It keeps your insides healthy.
filament	Part of the flower that holds the anther.
flowering plant	A plant that has flowers.
food group	An important substance found in foods. They include carbohydrates, proteins, fat, fibre, vitamins and minerals.
freeze	A liquid turning into a solid.
fruit (***froot***)	Part of a plant made from a flower that has seeds.
full moon	When the Moon looks like a complete circle.
gas	A substance that can spread all around us. We cannot see most gases. A gas fills its container, does not keep its volume and will flow.
germination (*jer-min-**ay**-shun*)	When a seed starts to grow.
gestation time (*jess-**tay**-shun*)	The scientific word for pregnancy.
gnomon (***no**-mon*)	The central stick in a sundial.
gram	The unit for measuring mass.
heart	An organ in your body which pumps blood.
heartbeat	Each time your heart contracts and then gets bigger again is called a heartbeat.
heart bypass operation	An operation where a person with a blocked coronary artery has a new piece of vein sewn in to bypass the blocked artery.
heart disease	When a small part of the heart has started to die.
helium (***hee**-lee-um*)	A gas found in the air. It is used in some balloons.
horizon (*hor-**I**-zon*)	The edge of the Earth that we can see.
illegal	If something is illegal the law says that you are not allowed to have it or do it.
impulses	Electrical signals.
joint	A part of the body where the bones can be moved by muscles.
kilojoules (kJ) (***kill**-O-jools*)	The units used to measure the amount of energy in food.
larynx (***larr**-inks*)	Part of the body that produces sounds and allows us to talk.
leap year	A year which has an extra day in it.
life cycle	The stages in a living thing's life. A life cycle starts when a living thing starts to grow and ends when it reproduces.
line graph	A graph with a line drawn through the points.
liquid (***lick**-wid*)	A substance that is runny and does not have a fixed shape. A liquid takes the shape of its container but keeps its volume and will flow.
loudspeaker	Something that converts electricity into sound.
mass	Something's mass is the amount of material it contains.
matter	Anything that takes up space is called matter.
medicine	A drug used to help people who are ill.
melt	A solid turning into a liquid.
melting	When a solid changes into a liquid.
mild	Weather that is neither very hot nor very cold.
minerals	A food group that is needed to keep you healthy.
muscle (***muss**-el*)	Part of the body that can contract (get shorter).
natural gas	A gas that is burnt for cooking and heating.
nectar	A sticky liquid that some flowers make to attract insects.
neon (***nee**-on*)	A gas that is in the air. It is used in signs which glow.
new moon	When you can hardly see the Moon at all.
nicotine (***nick**-O-teen*)	An addictive drug in cigarettes.
nitrogen (***nye**-trow-gen*)	A gas that makes up the biggest part of air.
North Pole	The place on the Earth that is further north than anywhere else.
nutrients (***new**-tree-ents*	Chemicals that living things need to grow.
observation (*ob-ser-**vay**-shun*)	Something you can see or measure. What you see happening in an experiment.
orbit	The path that the Earth follows around the Sun. When a planet moves around the Sun, or a moon moves around a planet.
organ	A part of any living thing which has a very important job.
ova	The plural of ovum.
ovary (***O**-very*)	Makes eggs in the flower.
ovum (***O**-vum*)	Female part of a plant which joins with a pollen grain in fertilisation. The plural is ova. Also called an egg.
oxygen (***oks**-ee-jen*)	A gas in the air which animals need to breathe.

petals	Brightly coloured parts of a flower.
phases of the Moon (*fay*-zes)	The different shapes that the Moon seems to be.
pigment	A coloured substance that gives paint its colour.
pinna	The outer flap of the ear which helps to funnel sounds into the ear.
pitch	How high or low a sound is.
pollen grain	Male part of a plant which joins with an ovum (egg) in fertilisation.
pollen tube	Tube which grows out of a pollen grain leading to the ovary.
pollination (poll-in-**ay**-shun)	When pollen grains land on a stigma.
predicting	Saying what you think will happen in an experiment.
prediction (pred-**ik**-shun)	Using scientific knowledge to say what you think will happen in an experiment and why.
pregnancy	When a female animal has a new baby growing inside her.
property	What something is like. For example, one property of solids is that they keep their shapes.
protein (**prO**-teen)	A food group that is needed to help you grow.
pulse	A wave of blood running through your arteries which you can feel at certain points on your body.
pulse rate	The number of times you can feel your pulse 'beat' in one minute.
relax	When a muscle relaxes it gets longer.
reproduce	When living things have young they are said to reproduce.
reservoir (**rez**-erv-wah)	An artificial lake made by damming a river.
ribcage	All your ribs make up your ribcage.
ribs	Bones which protect the heart and lungs.
runners	Little shoots that come out of a plant and grow along the soil. New plants grow out of the runners.
scurvy	A disease that makes your legs swell up, your gums bleed and your teeth fall out.
seed	It is made in the flower of a plant and can grow into a new plant.
seed dispersal (diss-**per**-sal)	Fruits are used to carry seeds (disperse them) away from where they are made. This can be done by animals, the wind, water or explosions.
seedling	A tiny new plant.
sepal	A part of a flower which protects it before it opens.
side-effect	An unpleasant effect of a medicine (e.g. giving you headaches).
solid	A solid keeps its shape and its volume, will not flow and is usually hard.
solvent abuse	Breathing in fumes from substances such as strong glues.
sphere (*s-fear*)	A round shape, like a football.
stamen (**stay**-men)	The male organ of the flower. It is made up of the anther and filament.
starch	A type of carbohydrate.
state	Whether a substance is a solid, a liquid or a gas.
states of matter	There are three forms or states of matter – solid, liquid and gas.
stigma	Where pollen grains land in a flower.
style	Joins the stigma to the ovary.
sugar	A type of carbohydrate. Sweet things contain a lot of sugar.
sundial	An instrument that allows you to tell the time using the Sun.
tar	A black chemical in cigarette smoke that causes lung cancer.
theory	A scientific idea that can be tested. A good theory can explain observations.
triceps (**try**-seps)	A muscle in your upper arm which contracts to lower your lower arm.
vein (*vane*)	A blood vessel carrying blood towards your heart.
vibrate (v-eye-**brate**)	Move backwards and forwards.
vibrations (v-eye-**bray**-shuns)	Movements backwards and forwards.
vitamins	A food group that is needed to keep you healthy. Vitamin C is an example.
vocal cords	Bands in the larynx that vibrate when we talk or sing.
volume	The amount of space something takes up.
water cycle	Water evaporates from the sea, condenses to form clouds, falls as rain, and eventually runs back to the sea again.
water vapour (**war**-ter **vay**-per)	Another name for water when it is a gas.
wind instrument	An instrument that you play by blowing, like a recorder or flute.
xenon (**zen**-on)	A gas that is in the air. It is used in some car headlights.
year	The length of time it takes for the Earth to go around the Sun once. A year lasts 365 days.